Praise for

The Conscience Economy
and Steven Overman

"Brilliant! Overman's keen observation of emerging trends in technology, social awareness, and astute consumerism deconstructs the tired canard that business is pitted against its community, employees, or society. *The Conscience Economy* objectively builds an overwhelming case that a company's brand derives its relevance, power, and vulnerability from the sum of the firm's actions."

—Jeff Clarke, CEO, Kodak

"A compelling read, like a travelogue full of observations that invite us to experience profound changes happening across different cultures around the world. Our company is focused on protecting and connecting people to the things that matter most, so Overman's connectivity points ring especially true for me. *The Conscience Economy* is full of provocative insights, fresh ideas, and practical advice for any business."

—Jerri DeVard, chief marketing officer, ADT Security

"I love the energy of *The Conscience Economy* and the inevitable truths that Overman so masterfully weaves into every page. Overman takes us on a journey into the myriad ways in which this growing awareness is already shaping our world and has the potential to create a new reality where every business conducts itself in a fundamentally different way. A must-read for everyone who is considering how they can steer themselves and their business towards a more sustainable and balanced world."

—Alex Willcock, CEO, VisualDNA

"*The Conscience Economy* makes a rich, compelling case for why it's no longer just enough to do *well*—if we want to succeed in life, we also have to do *good*. Whether you're motivated by conscience or profit, this book will show you how you can tap into the Conscience Economy to grow your business, create a positive impact in the world, and wake up smiling." —Nathalie Nahai, author, *Webs of Influence*

The
Conscience
Economy

The Conscience Economy

HOW A MASS MOVEMENT FOR GOOD
IS GREAT FOR BUSINESS

Steven Overman

bibliomotion
books + media

First published by Bibliomotion, Inc.

39 Harvard Street
Brookline, MA 02445
Tel: 617-934-2427
www.bibliomotion.com

Printed in the United States of America

Library of Congress Cataloging-in-Publication Data

Overman, Steven.
   The conscience economy : how a mass movement for good is great for business / Steven Overman.
     pages cm
   Summary: "The Conscience Economy will help international leaders, influencers, investors and decision-makers to manage, innovate and thrive in a new world where "doing good" matters as mush as "doing well.""—Provided by publisher.
   ISBN 978-1-62956-012-0 (hardback) — ISBN 978-1-62956-013-7 (ebook) — ISBN 978-1-62956-014-4 (enhanced ebook)
   1. Social responsibility of business.   2. Social entrepreneurship.   3. Economic development—Social aspects.   I. Title.
   HD60.O93 2014
   658.4'08—dc23
                              2014023615

For Lily, who will inherit the future we all create

Contents

Foreword

By Louis Rossetto

I was at a dinner in Cambridge, Massachusetts, recently with a dozen Harvard/MIT/Princeton faculty/researchers/directors. Very bright, very switched on people involved in important, even groundbreaking, work.

About dessert time, the discussion coalesced to the big question that inevitably haunts big thinkers: How do we solve the really big problems? Everyone was depressed that life on the planet was obviously getting worse. And they were frustrated, even angry, that the legacy players were failing. Why wasn't Obama able to solve our problems? The UN? The World Bank? The Gates Foundation?

I wish Steven Overman had been at my side at that dinner, as he was during the early days at *Wired* in the '90s. At *Wired*, we created a unique intelligence operation masquerading as a magazine that reported on the exploding Digital Revolution. Our specialty was roaming across the horizon of the future and bringing back fresh kill for our readers. We jokingly called it Revolution of the Month—so much of the world was being remade, from business to politics, from education to entertainment, from energy to health, from religion to sex—as the middlemen were disintermediated and power devolved as digital tools became more widespread and influential. We embraced this revolution with optimism: our motto was Change Is Good.

But we didn't just report on the revolution, we helped make it happen. At *Wired*, we pioneered web media, creating the first website with original content and Fortune 500 advertising. We invented the banner ad, and then helped start an agency to sell and create those ads, because it didn't exist yet. Wired Ones launched the first blog as we now know it, setting off the earthquake that traditional journalism never recovered from. We created the first website, the *Netizen*, that reported on a presidential election. Then we fought the government's attempt to spy on citizens' and businesses' communications via the Clipper chip, and became named plaintiffs in the lawsuit that overturned the unconstitutional Communications Decency Act.

From *Wired*, Steven went on to spread the Digital Revolution across the planet, helping to build what was, at the time, the biggest, most innovative cell phone company in the world. So when he speaks of change, he speaks from a position of authority as one who has been in the trenches of the revolution from San Francisco to cyberspace, from Helsinki to Mumbai, from Beijing to Cape Town.

It's little wonder I wish Steven had been at that dinner. He would have taken strong exception to the guests' pessimism and told them, wait, in the first place, all metrics indicate that the world isn't getting worse, it's actually getting better, even if problems remain. And that yes, while the legacy players may be failing, a new paradigm is emerging that offers the possibility of making an even better world.

Then Steven would have raised the real question everyone should have been asking that night, which isn't "How do we solve the really big problems?" but "Just who is this 'we'?" For Steven, the "we" isn't the government, the NGOs, or the supra-national institutions, which are becoming increasingly ineffectual and, dare we say it, obsolete. The "we" is, in fact, *us*.

Because in the twenty-first century, as Steven points out in his illuminating and provocative new book, "we"—each of us as individuals, family members, employees, entrepreneurs, managers, citizens, and consumers—are together not only assuming the responsibility for making a better world, we have acquired the power to do it directly. And the economy is reshaping itself around that reality. Steven calls it the Conscience Economy.

The signs, Steven points out, are all around us. Companies are reshaping themselves to be more responsible, value-driven, and transparent, proudly telling us how their product is made, that they are good custodians of the environment, that their relationships with all their stakeholders are ethical. In effect, they are internalizing conscience as an integral part of their business practices, and they are informing consumers about it in their advertising and marketing, and on the labels of the products they sell—and not because of government pressure, but because doing good is actually good business. Or as Steven puts it: "Goodness is the wellspring of profit."

And it's a good thing *The Conscience Economy* is so compelling because, as Steven argues, we absolutely need it. The networked planet forces us to know more about what's going on everywhere than we ever did—we can't avoid the truth. And one of truths we can't avoid is that remote political and philanthropic institutions aren't cutting it anymore. So if we want to make a better future for our children, we can't outsource that responsibility the way we used to, we have to assume it ourselves, personally. Disintermediation reaches the civic space.

Though it is a stirring call to consciousness, *The Conscience Economy* is cool because most of it is a lively report from the future that is expressing itself in today's business environment. Discover for yourself: crowdifying; why corporate social responsibility and marketing are both dead (Revolution of the Month, indeed), the 5Cs of marketing, and how CMO doesn't mean chief marketing officer, but chief matchmaking officer—among countless other revelations and insights in Steven's book.

Steven's *The Conscience Economy* makes one other contribution. In a period suffused with entirely too much unjustified pessimism spread by legacy media that make money fostering mass anxiety, *The Conscience Economy* is a refreshing blast of unabashed optimism, complete with a scenario for a utopian future (which you, like I, will want to challenge in places, but that's what a book like *The Conscience Economy* is supposed to do, provoke discussion).

Steven is optimistic not because optimism is nice, but because he knows, as we used to argue at *Wired*, that optimism is a strategy for living.

If you're pessimistic about the future, you're likely to embrace an *après moi le déluge* attitude and focus on short-term gratification. On the other hand, if you believe the future will be better, you will step up, take responsibility, and do the long-term thinking necessary to make that better world for you and your children. So, solving those big problems my dinner guests were obsessing about starts not with doom and gloom, but with optimism.

The Conscience Economy has arrived at precisely the right moment, and Steven Overman is its herald. Be optimistic like Steven. He has seen the future, and it works.

Louis Rossetto
Co-founder Wired, a disruptive media company
Co-founder TCHO, a disruptive chocolate company

Berkeley
2014.07.11

Introduction

Good Is the New Bad

It's midmorning and the temperature has already climbed above eighty degrees. I'm driving a rental car down a sun-drenched Florida freeway, the air conditioning cranked way up while a friendly Google Maps voice directs me past vast, car-dependent housing developments, giant-box retail outlets, Spanish Colonial–style multiplex cinemas, and tall groves of billboards proclaiming miracles of modern cardiology. The air is thick with humidity, the landscape watery, flat, and punctuated with palm trees, stretching for miles at what seems like a mere six inches above sea level. It occurs to me that this scene—with its infinite, built-yesterday sprawl—is the expression of centuries of human dreams and desires. For millions, this is paradise.

This being Florida, and South Florida in particular, it is also the end of the road. North America's retirement mecca. I'm tempted to milk the scenario for some kind of ironic connection between an unsustainable way of life and the end of life. But it's simultaneously the beginning of a new road, an extension of Latin America's energetic, youthful optimism. There's no clever metaphor here, I realize: this isn't only how life is laid out in a subtropical peninsula known for its high proportion of retirees and immigrants. This is all of America, land of convenience and home of immediate gratification, and much of the world wants to get in on it.

Surrounded with this kind of accessible and reasonably low-cost abundance, it's hard to imagine that attitudes and desires will ever change.

For one thing, so much of the physical infrastructure of contemporary life seems permanently fixed. But the dreams and motivations that drove the creation of this asphalt and petroleum-dependent infrastructure *are* changing—and fast.

A new generation aspires to something different, and they're making everyday choices in ways that defy traditional logic. They're rejecting the old norms—because they can. They're questioning everything from the notion of career consistency to the value of money itself. They're hacking everything from government policy to the genome.

They are judging where and how their clothes are made, not just how they fit. They are creating and broadcasting their own media, expressing their points of view, and boycotting and endorsing companies based on their own values. They are thinking global but buying local and, if they can, fair trade and slavery free. They are using mobile phones to overthrow their governments. They are creating social enterprises and investment funds for social progress. They are spending their money and their time forming loyalties, casting votes, and even enjoying entertainment based increasingly upon their desire to make a positive impact on others and the world around them.

The once quaintly idealistic motivation to make a positive impact on the world has thrown off its unbleached, woven-hemp cloak of hippie self-righteousness. Today, enlightenment is downright sexy. It's taken on an aura of forward-thinking chic, even as it's becoming increasingly mainstream. From setting up a third wave coffee shop to founding a social enterprise to paving a rooftop with solar panels, doing good is the new status symbol—or, as a trendsetting hipster would say, at least at the time of this writing, doing good is *totally badass*.

This new generation believes they can and *must* make the world better, and they expect business and government to get with the program.

Let's face it, in business it has long been smart, if not exactly nice, to exploit natural resources and low-cost workers for profit. Good business, more often than not, required a measure of bad behavior, at least from an environmental and social perspective. The strong business leader, willing to make the tough decisions, was typically or at least visibly unconcerned about anything but the bottom line, even at the expense of humanity and our planet. After all, there was always philanthropy to assuage any nagging guilt and whitewash a reputation. Backslapping (or backstabbing) cliches abound: good guys finish last, no good deed goes unpunished, you're swimming with the sharks, don't take it personally because it's only business.

Business badness was more than profitable, it could even be admirable, as long as you didn't get caught. Even celebrities—our collective role models—could be deliciously naughty, whether it was a certain iconic songster's rumored connections to organized crime or a rock band's legendary destruction of their hotel room. Bad behavior—and particularly, getting away with bad behavior—has long been a fertile source of value share. But the emergent culture, including increasing numbers of business leaders, has a different idea about what's radical, edgy, smart, and valuable.

The visible and most obvious examples are legion. Here's a back-of-the-envelope list:

- The global wave of young entrepreneurship is an indicator not only of an increase in personal self-belief and empowerment, but a sign of the growing optimism that there could and will be a better way to work, produce, and live.

- We are what we eat, and buying locally sourced and organic produce and meat is no longer solely the province of a niche segment of elitist customers—it's one of the fastest-growing categories in food, while traditional fast food and sweetened carbonated beverages are seeing their profits stumble as they hit a plateau in developed markets.

- Our favorite celebrities make films about topical issues, rebuild homes in flood-ravaged communities, and stand up for urgent global causes, while promoting healthy nutrition.

- Social enterprises—organizations that have as their core purpose generating a healthy profit by innovating for the benefit of the greater good—are the hottest category of start-up today, attracting both private and public investment and top talent.

- Impact investing—which creates funds, frameworks, and financial instruments that put capital to work for the greater good while generating a competitive return—continues to gain momentum and clout in the financial industry.

- Mainstream media debate the role of humans—and by default, the role of business—in the seemingly endless spate of extreme weather.

- The next wave of mobile technology innovation is being driven by a proliferation of patents in biometric sensors that have the power to virtualize health-care diagnostic procedures, driving down costs and expanding health-care accessibility and efficacy.
- Companies manufacturing everything from apparel to microchips band together in industry coalitions that create and enforce codes of conduct to improve the health and safety of their workers and stabilize the communities in which they operate.
- Marriage equality spreads from state to state with the vocal support of companies that have long offered domestic partnership benefits to their employees.
- A proliferation of new web-based and mobile services enable regular people—amateurs—to monetize the empty passenger seats in their cars and the empty beds in their guest rooms, thereby maximizing the economic efficiency of limited resources like fuel and living space while creating value and building personal social relationships.
- The court of real-time public opinion stretches around the globe, with more people more empowered than ever before. Broad boycotts of companies because of the political views of their leaders—and heartfelt personal promotions of companies with values in sync with those of their public—spread across the social graph at the speed of one hundred forty per tweet.
- Microloans and crowdfunding enable new, often socially motivated businesses to sprout from anywhere, democratizing investment and entrepreneurship like never before. At the same time, they create virtual stakeholder relationships and shared accountability for results between individuals who formerly wouldn't have had access to one another.
- Companies that make products and services that empower individual creativity and knowledge—Apple and Google—top the list in brand value, while the technology category overall is the most admired business sector.
- The idea of true cost economics has moved from an online manifesto to an academically endorsed concept to the driver of a new and fast-growing movement toward integrated financial reporting in the accounting industry.

Here's the great news: this massive shift—in society, life, work, and especially business—offers an unprecedented opportunity for all of us to prosper, grow, find greater happiness, and transform the world for the better.

Here's the harder news: none of us is ready for it. Business especially. And this is ironic, because it is we businesspeople who have catalyzed this change.

We are entering a moment of social and technological disruption that most businesses simply weren't built to accommodate. Business as we know it is based upon a set of implied and in many cases explicit rules and principles, ensconced not only in years of business practice but also in academia and law. These are being upended by a value system, and the technology to support it, that has been steadily moving from the margin to the mainstream for decades. Indeed, we are reaching a tipping point in our evolution as a global society.

Accuse me of overstatement, but the rules and principles that have long underpinned our received logic of business, society, economics, and life are being turned upside down. The evidence is not only all around you. It's *in* you. You wouldn't be reading these words if you didn't have a gut feeling that we're living and working in a time of great disruption. Debates about the future viability of capitalism, the emergence of socially enabled media, entertainment, education, and even money, the increasing volume of concern that cataclysmic environmental consequences could be imminent if we don't change our ways, rapid advances in artificial intelligence and robotics, the potential impact of genetic engineering, the way that smartphones are transforming how we do just about everything, food safety and food security concerns, dialogue about the future of the Internet itself and whom it's really serving—contemporary life is full of big and real questions about the future we are creating for ourselves.

The old ways of operating an enterprise—from leadership to product and service innovation to talent management, marketing, sales, and distribution—are hitting their expiration dates. No matter how enlightened or progressive we may be as individuals and leaders, most business processes have fallen out of sync with an emerging value system that not only expects but loudly demands transparency, authenticity, democracy, collaboration, empowerment, and fairness—all while serving the best interests of individual human rights, healthy societies, and a thriving natural environment.

Meanwhile, for more people than ever before, business is a bad word. And we're not just talking about the banking sector, which you won't be surprised to learn is for most people the lowest of the low, mistrusted by 96 percent of customers around the world, according to a recent Futures Company global survey on trust in business. People increasingly express a deepening disappointment with business as an entire category of human endeavor. What you and I (and indeed even they, the mistrusting masses) do every day, all of our sweat and tears and often good intentions, according to a majority of people around the world, is little more than a necessary evil.

Of course, people not only depend upon but even fall madly in love with products that can only be created by big business. But these feelings don't necessarily extend to the companies that make said objects of affection. And increasingly, how people feel about *companies* is having an impact on the choices they make. Company reputation and brand loyalty are more codependent than ever before.

Let's admit that much of the ill will directed at business is deserved. The deep damage of financial crises, fatalities from unsafe factory conditions, and the long-term effects of environmental exploitation are more than valid reasons for mistrust and even rage. That old "me, the humble citizen" versus "they, the powerful businesspeople" dialectic is nearing the end of its lifespan.

"The corporation is just a machine," a colleague recently said to me when I described an unfortunate work circumstance that left me personally disappointed. Despite my own occasional frustrations, I disagree with this oft-said and well-intentioned sentiment. To state the obvious, businesses of all sizes—even giant "faceless" corporations—are comprised of people and thus businesses are ultimately, and fallibly, human. Sometimes, when you put a lot of people together and the stakes are high, humans aren't at their best. Many little mistakes get magnified into catastrophic consequences. Business failure is human failure.

Still, just as humanity is not inherently evil, neither is business. Indeed, if it has the power to hurt, it has even more power to help. The magnifying, exponential effects of large groups of well-intentioned human beings working in concert can be, and have been at many moments in business history, a force for good. In the mid-nineteenth century, some of the most successful and fast-growing businesses in Britain (and it bears remembering that at the time Britain's economy was not only the largest in Europe, it was larger than that of the United States) were run by Quakers who, because of their religion, were excluded from much of elite society, and thus channeled their lives into enterprise where they could put their values into practice. Companies like Cadbury and Rowntree, for example, ran their businesses while offering what were at the time unparalleled provisions (housing, health care) for not only their workers but also the broader communities in which they operated. In the 1980s, companies like The Body Shop put the notion of cruelty-free production into mainstream consciousness. Broad business sanctions against South Africa helped put the final nail in the coffin of apartheid.

The role of business in driving positive change is set to increase. As Niall FitzGerald, former chairman and CEO of Unilever, stated in a report called *The Role of Business in Society,* "This challenge to business leaders—to identify with society in tackling the social and environmental problems of globalization, not just through philanthropy, but by using their innovative and creative capabilities to find business solutions that contribute to solving these problems—is the challenge of the twenty-first century. And it is a challenge to all of us engaged in the market economy."

To what can we attribute this shift, this disruption, this next big step forward? We can thank technology, which really means looking in the mirror and thanking ourselves for not only creating but also enthusiastically adopting technology so wholeheartedly into nearly every area of our lives. The Internet has not only brought people closer together, it's brought people and business closer together too. The world is not only more connected (and more crowded), it has become a far more intimate place than ever before.

Is this a blessing? Or does it present a more complicated set of operating circumstances for the enterprise? We can and do proclaim the wonders of deeper customer engagement, the freedom and productivity that mobility provides the enterprise, and the convenience of more efficiently distributed communication, but what's also true is that this new intimacy is uncomfortable. We're not used to it. Business as we currently conduct it, and business value as we currently create, measure, and report it, is not based on deep intimacy but rather on separateness. Opacity. But no, you're thinking, we *aspire* to become more intimate with our customers. I'm sure you do; so do I. Rousing PowerPoint presentations and social media proposals extolling the virtues of closer connections between a business and its customers abound. You want to know *everything* about them, but do you want them to know *everything* about you? For example, do you want your customers to know what you're really doing with what you know about them? After all, intimacy is a two-way street.

Frankly, whatever business wants, it has no choice but to be more open than is currently comfortable. The walls are coming down. The disintermediation, virtualization, and automation of the digital revolution have already swept through nearly every known business model. That was only the beginning of the transformation. The accelerating pace of social change, continuous economic volatility, wildly swinging extremes of consumer demand, and the subsequent redistribution of power from the few to the many: these phenomena are gathering pace as more and more of humanity come online. Whatever you believe about income inequality and the popular notion that wealth is being transferred into the hands of a smaller percentage of people, wealth is indeed a form of power. Some theorists, like Thomas Piketty in his critique of capitalism itself, argue that today it's being concentrated in an ever smaller proportion of people at a historically unprecedented rate. Yet paradoxically—and in the long run, perhaps more significantly—more people have more choice, more agency, more information, more opportunity to participate, more ability to join forces with like minds, and an unlimited audience for their ideas and personal and political expression. This too is power. And it is spreading to more people than ever.

Think about it. Throughout human history, people were disconnected from one another and the wider world by vast spans of geographic space and travel time. The pursuit of global trade and the institutions that dominated it created connections around the globe, but until very recently this connectivity was slow, expensive, and accessible only to the elite. It's easy to forget that being separate was simply an ontological reality.

Centuries of separateness—despite our growing global economic interdependence—put in place and ossified whole systems based on impenetrable boundaries. Boundaries of information. Boundaries of power. Business value and profit margin were not only based on supply and demand, but upon manipulating what information the buyer could access. The idea was to produce at the lowest possible price and charge the highest possible price. Logical. Because the buyer had no way of knowing the real cost of goods, and even if she had a way to figure it out, there wasn't much she could do about it. Despite the notion that pricing is based on "what the market will bear," in the short-term game of supply-side economics, value was set by the producer. Ultimately, value was dependent upon *opacity*.

So what happens when more of us are more connected to one another and to everything in real time than ever before? What happens when business opacity—like privacy—evaporates? Before we continue our well-justified love affair with connectivity, it's worth pausing to consider just how profound this new reality is. Because in just a few short decades, ubiquitous connectivity has gone from a seemingly magical innovation to a basic utility, and it's not slowing down—it's speeding up.

For those businesses that adapt to this shift in values, the ones that address people's hopes and expectations head-on and that truly deliver what people want and need (and isn't that the whole point of business?) at this moment in time, what may look like a crisis is indeed the best opportunity we've been presented to innovate, create sustainable value, and grow.

Global interdependence—and the emergent values and expectations that such interdependence generates—is not just a here-today-gone-next-quarter trend. Nor is it a left-of-center or libertarian political movement or a set of unrealistic utopian ideals that are getting more than their fair share of airplay online. The conversation about the role of business in society is escalating across the political spectrum. Meanwhile, making a corporate commitment to generating positive social and environmental impact is no longer merely a nice thing for a business to do to improve its reputation; it's becoming acknowledged as a future-friendly, pragmatic, and increasingly urgent business imperative. Prioritizing the common good as a core purpose—and the institutional transformation required in order to fulfill this purpose—is spreading through every realm of human endeavor, from politics to health care to international policy to finance. But it is business that will be both most affected and simultaneously the most powerful actor and influencer, because it's business that has so much to gain from the opportunities this unique inflection point offers.

This inflection point, this cultural shift toward an economics rooted in the common good is a multidimensional phenomenon, encompassing individual motivations and beliefs, communal values, technological capabilities, scientific and biological evidence, and global geopolitical dilemmas. The converging shifts in these various business drivers herald the emergence of a new economic paradigm based on redefined ideas of utility, demand, and stakeholder accountability.

A word about corporate responsibility (there's a whole chapter on it later). If you're anything like me, you probably have mixed feelings about the word "responsible," as in environmentally responsible, socially responsible. It's patronizing and infantilizing and, frankly, unfriendly. Let's aim instead to be *sensible*. As in environmentally sensible, socially sensible. It's not sensible for businesses to pollute our precious water supply. It's not sensible for businesses to put their workers and the communities in which they operate at risk. It's not sensible to lie to customers, even if it's a lie by withholding the truth. It's not sensible for businesses to allow destabilizing political conflicts to fester and grow, inhibiting their ability to produce and sell.

Here's an uncomfortable paradox that I by no means morally endorse: it might well be sensible in the short term for an individual to exploit resources and other people in his or her own (unenlightened) self-interest, if he or she is a sociopath or a power-hungry politician. But for businesses, which depend on healthy and financially solvent customers, market stability, and sustainable and steady growth, it's simply irrational. Investors, who by definition must balance both the short and long view, seek evidence of longer-term stability and predictable growth against the backdrop of continuous volatility, so with growth in mind, it's logical that a longer view must ultimately prevail without jeopardizing short-term profit and thus viability. But it's not just about investors. Long-term viability is an increasing priority within the enterprise. Part of Unilever's business, for example, depends upon sustainable fish stocks. So the business has partnered with the World Wide Fund for Nature (WWF) to ensure sustainability standards that aim to protect this natural (and, it must be said, business) resource.

A connected world is a smarter world, and a smarter world is an empowered world. As more of us become more closely linked to one another, to information, and to the realities around us—realities both challenging and hopeful—our awareness of our own impact on the world continues to grow. Over time, this growing awareness has become converted into action. We know we can't let things keep going as they have been. We share an increasingly crowded planet, and its capacity to support and extend our current way of life is under strain. We know we can't keep living and working as we have been. It's unsustainable, and it's not sensible. So we won't do it.

A new era of real-time knowledge and pragmatic reciprocity is dawning. If we treat ourselves to the privilege of leaving cynicism behind for a moment, it's not unimaginable that an age of near-universal and rampant profiteering from bad behavior, exploiting human beings and natural resources with abandon, could one day come to a close. After all, business is made of people and natural resources, and it is no longer sensible to extract margin from damaging that upon which we depend.

Brand loyalty and the value it delivers will no longer emanate from manipulating people into paying more, contributing to your margin by obfuscating the truth. No longer can business seduce hearts and wallets to open with false promises to fulfill fabricated desires. Authenticity and transparency are winning the race. New, truth-based approaches to brand building and engaging those who are most likely to buy your product will be core competitive advantages going forward, as we'll see in both chapters 4 and 6.

Business has the most to gain by driving change, because government intervention compelled by populist movements (the rising tide of resentment of executive compensation, for example) could be a very scary thing indeed for businesses. Guardrails are good, but for those who believe in the power of the free market (full disclosure: I do), too much regulatory intervention demotivates business performance. At the same time, government and public institutions have a crucial role to play in protecting communities as well as property rights, and ensuring personal freedom. Government-funded innovation is a crucial component in human progress. The world's most valuable innovations—the Internet being the most obvious but not the only example—simply did not emerge purely from the private sector. They were built on the back of systems and discoveries that were government funded.

Business may well have been the modern agent of many of the dilemmas we face. It will also be the most powerful agent in solving them. Because that which is valuable should be profitable. What could be more valuable than making life safer, better, and longer for all humanity? What could be more valuable than continually restoring the health and vitality of our planet, the only inhabitable home in the universe?

Every business wants to get ahead of the next big thing. This is it. Welcome to the Conscience Economy.

1

From Conscious to Conscience

It's 9:15 on a Thursday night and I'm leaning against the bar in a hip and underlit restaurant that sits between London's sleek and shiny financial district and its up-and-coming "Silicon Roundabout," a gritty traffic interchange speckled with both start-ups and Google offices. As candles flicker, the room buzzes with animated conversations, plates and silverware clatter, and cocktail shakers make their steady "ch-ch-ch-ch." I take in the scene, one that's replicated in conurbations of human talent, capital flow, and privilege around the world, from Singapore to Paris to Dubai to New York. It occurs to me that I could at this moment be anywhere, as I try to count the number of languages I hear, as I catalog the different accents of English that surround me.

And that's when I hear it. A line that sums up ten years of observation, thinking, and, dare I admit it, hope. A sentence that articulates why I felt compelled to write this book.

They're sitting to my left, a few barstools away. It's obviously a date. She's poised and attentive in her special-night-out black dress, hair in a perfect knot. He's almost breathless with enthusiasm in his attractively rumpled been-in-meetings-all-day business clothes. He's telling her all about his new company. Big grin, big gestures. Leaning in. He's got the confidence of a classic Young Turk, one of those good-looking, well-presenting, high-potential guys in their late twenties. In equal parts irritating and admirable, he's the kind of guy I know the venture capitalists love, because he seems by his demeanor alone that he could be the next Sergei or Larry or Steve. He oozes charisma. And although his date has surely seen this kind of chutzpah before, she's listening closely. As am I. As he says these words.

"We've just closed another nine million in financing. And you know why that makes me so proud? Because we're not just doing *well*. We're doing *good*."

Roll your eyes if you will. (Though if you're reading this book I'm pretty sure you'd agree with our Young Turk. Let's call him YT.) But this impress-the-date comment is heartfelt. And YT keeps going, beaming with pride as he explains the complexities and challenges of his business, which, from what I can hear, provides some kind of infrastructure technology that will make everyday energy utilities more sustainable and carbon efficient. If what he's sketching out during this romantic interlude (it wasn't only the young woman who was captivated at this point) actually succeeds, he will indeed be doing well *and* doing good. It's hard to be cynical when his earnestness for doing the right thing, while getting millions of dollars invested in doing it, is real.

But here's the better reason to eavesdrop. Not because he's unusual or provocative. Quite the opposite. The mind-set and attitude of our "change the world" YT is surprisingly unexceptional. He's typical of his generation. Understanding the emergent mind-set he represents will open doors to new opportunities for creating value and positive change. Who doesn't want to do that?

To cite an obvious and blunt example, consider the mass of young people who created a revolution—and may yet do it again—with mobile phones and Facebook accounts in Tahrir Square. Consider the hordes of church youth groups who've flocked halfway across the U.S. to rebuild towns devastated by tornadoes and hurricanes. Monitor the comments on Instagram, Facebook, Twitter, and YouTube, on every topic from war to marriage equality to gender to the environment. Empowerment and connectedness are fueling a reordering of assumptions and priorities. When something as profound as a generational mind-set is transforming on a mass scale, it's wise to take note. Revolutions sweep through societal norms, business models, and consumer expectations as well as governments. Just ask anyone in the music industry.

Back to our guy at the bar. Though he might look the same, in fact he's rather unlike the generation (mine, generation X) that preceded him.

Something Different in the Air

Just for fun, let's time travel. Let's visit YT's predecessor in *his* heyday.

The scene: hip-and-underlit designer martini and pizza bar, but in a different city. Let's say San Francisco, circa 1998. The din is the same: cocktail shaker "ch-ch-ch-ch," the cacophony of conversation, bullish confidence in the air.

But the words are different. Very different. "Dotcom." "Valuation." "IPO." "Exit strategy."

Our late '90s YT is a different animal. I worked with him, and with her. Lots of them, actually.

The primary motivation then? Simple. Get rich, as quickly as possible. Work the system at any cost and get out of it with a high-speed vesting schedule while laughing your way to the real estate agents. At the time, I was working with a typical San Francisco start-up, and I had suggested taking "dotcom" out of the company's name. I remember during one conversation about it, a bullish colleague said to me, "It doesn't matter what our business model really is in the end. Let's just keep dotcom in the name so we keep our valuation high."

Six months later, of course, the dotcom bubble burst. That's when I finally won the argument. But we all lost the company. So many start-up dreams blazed like fireworks, and like fireworks they simply dissolved into thin air.

That was then. There's something different in the air now.

Let's cut to the present again. This time, to a very different scene.

I'm in Soweto, the Johannesburg township that gave rise and voice to some of the greatest emancipators in a generation: Desmond Tutu, Nelson Mandela. I've traveled here with some of my colleagues to learn firsthand how life is for young people in this inspiring but challenging nation. After the obligatory ride past Tutu's and Mandela's now-enshrined homes, and after kicking a football around in the baking sunshine with some of the local young people to break the ice, my colleagues and I are visiting what Mangaliso, the young man in front of me, calls his "concept store," smack in the heart of the township.

What is a "concept store"? It's a retail environment that doesn't specialize in one kind of product but instead sells a lifestyle by selecting and presenting a range of different types of products that all have a theme (a concept, if you will) in common.

Prior to my field trip to Soweto, I'd only visited one other concept store: Colette, on rue Saint-Honoré in Paris. At Colette, the concept on display is edgy, fashionable irony. You can browse through racks of triple-digit-price tag Day-Glo tee shirts, limited edition Coca-Cola bottles (matte white!), and small-batch perfumes (smells like hot asphalt!) that you wouldn't find anywhere else. All of which express a certain uniquely Parisian je ne sais quoi of style and savoir faire. You could, I suppose, accuse such an environment of being elitist. Except that unlike at, say, Chanel, even a fourth grader with milk money could afford something in Colette. Perhaps a Rubik's Cube key ring or a funky plastic bracelet. She just needs to know where to go and what's cool to buy. Price isn't the point. That's a concept store. It's about being in the know.

So what is a "concept store" doing in an economically deprived albeit famous township in Johannesburg? And what on earth is it selling?

Mangaliso starts to explain. He's addicted to international lifestyle magazines, and he surfs the web on his iPhone searching for new ideas from around the world. He's never been outside South Africa, and rarely has he even left the township, at least not physically. But he is well aware of Colette in Paris, of the influence that the store exerts on the world as a trendsetter, and he wants to do the same with his neighbors. And so, with his friends, he has opened his own concept store in what can only be described as a large shed on a dusty road under the simmering African sky, and the concept that his store sells can be summed up, like so many of the best ideas, on a tee shirt.

From a rack, he pulls one—extra large, to fit me I assume—emblazoned with a comic book–style illustration of a knot and two hands creating the shape of a heart. There's an African word above the illustration. "This," he proclaims, "is what we're all about. *Ubuntu.*"

The Ubuntu Mind-Set

Ubuntu is a Zulu term that roughly translates as "human kindness through togetherness." Wikipedia does it more justice than I can here.

Suffice it to say, ubuntu describes the worldview that each of us is manifest through all of us. I am me because of you. We need each other in order to be ourselves. We have a metaphysical obligation to overcome tribal or prejudicial difference by joining together into one humanity that expresses only kindness. This is the key to our strength and our survival.

Mangaliso explains all of this to me in the matter-of-fact way you might describe, say, how to download an app to your tablet. As he walks me through his merchandise, from apparel to silk-screened artworks, he tells me how the store has become a social hub for the young people in the township. He tells me how, together, he and his neighbors throw impromptu parties, how they inspire young people in the township and beyond to create products of their own that express ubuntu, because now there's a place to sell them. It's more than a store. It's a social catalyst. And in time, I suspect, an economic catalyst in his community too.

Ubuntu. This is a big concept. Indeed, concepts don't really get much bigger, or frankly, more relevant, and not only in South Africa. Here's our young shopkeeper with his eagle eye on the global marketplace of ideas, selling it on tee shirts, homemade magazines, skateboards, hats, parties. An internationally resonant philosophy that's productized, designed locally, made locally, sold locally. This could be the birth of a great brand.

My colleagues and I try to buy out the whole store, but we realize that it might impact his mission, so we leave about half of his stock behind, a decision that now, as I type this, I regret. What he's doing seems profound, while simultaneously it's very hip. It's social media made into matter. And his mission is emblematic of his generation, a cohort of around-the-world under-thirties that marketers refer to as millennials, a group that have grown up with Internet connectivity and have only ever known a world to which they are digitally and wholly connected. A group that feels they have not only the power but the responsibility to make a difference.

One more snapshot from the present:

I'm visiting Delhi, where I'm getting to know some more of these millennials, but in a different context. This time, I've been invited to spend an afternoon with some young people who live in a fifth-floor walk-up apartment in a bustling neighborhood of Delhi. As we pull up outside the apartment building, an emaciated cow saunters by. Dogs lie asleep in the shade of market stalls piled high with mangoes. People whizz past on bicycles, rickshaws, motorbikes, belching trucks, and packed mini-buses. Life in Delhi is a nonstop churn of energy. It's not a carefree place, but it's full of surprising paradoxes, and it's vibrant with humanity. But nothing I've read or have been told has prepared me for the humanity of the conversation I'm about to have.

We're meeting two friends, Raghuvesh and Amit. Raghuvesh lives here with his family, and he ushers me into a spotlessly clean front room lit with a single fluorescent bulb. There's just enough space for two small wooden chairs, a bench, and a table that can hold, barely, four cups of tea. My eyes dart around the worn walls, looking for anything familiar, anything that's something like my own living room. This home could not be more different from my own.

But the smiles we exchange are universal, and our conversation begins. I'm particularly interested in how these two guys—my lanky host is twenty years old, his friend is seventeen—feel about technology and their own futures. After some typical sentiments ("I can't be without my cellphone..." "I'm very busy with my studies because I want to be successful...") the discussion shifts to entrepreneurship—which to me is surprising. India's deeply entrenched caste system is emblematic of a hierarchical society. In the very recent past, a young man like Raghuvesh would expect to start at the bottom of an established or family business and work his way up, at least as far as his caste would allow him to go.

But Raghuvesh has a different notion of his own future. He speaks softly, but with the assurance of his own conviction. "I will be my own boss. I want to start a company, so I can create opportunities for Amit, and for my other friends."

"For your friends?" I ask.

Raghuvesh glances at his cellphone, then looks up again and smiles at me. "I would do anything for my friends, because I love them. Whatever happens to them happens to me. What's good for them is good for me, and good for my family. It would be good to be in charge of our own future, and to make it happen together."

Now, to a non-Indian, perhaps Raghuvesh sounds amazingly emo-tionally evolved, especially for his gender. How many American twenty-year-old guys are so comfortable using the word "love" when talking about their friends? So it bears noting that India, like China and other emerging-market societies, tends to prioritize the community over the individual. And in India, the spiritual and the everyday are more interwoven than in any other culture I've encountered; indeed it is often said that Hinduism itself (one of a dozen faith traditions that suffuse the subcontinent) is more a way of life and a worldview than a religion per se. But this doesn't account for Raghuvesh's next statement. "I want to make a difference, and I believe that I can. We need to take responsibility for our future. My generation will make things happen together."

There is a fusion of forces electrifying the mind-set I am encountering in this humble apartment. I've encountered it before, in other humble rooms in burgeoning cities across the developing world. This combination of community responsibility, global Internet connectivity, and the aspiration to entrepreneurship is no longer the sole province of the privileged American West Coast university graduate.

It's so obvious that it almost blends into the background of contemporary life. But when you open your ears, this refrain of "I want to make a difference, because I can" is everywhere. From an exclusive London boîte to a dusty Soweto shed to a sitting room in Delhi.

Something has changed. A new imperative dominates conversations and decisions. It seems that around the world, there's been some soul-searching. The planet has gradually but steadily been developing a conscience.

Life Begins at Forty

Sociologists have identified an intriguing pattern in broad cultural change, and it is this: most inventions or big ideas take approximately forty years to move from the margins to the mainstream. In other words, the maturation and spread of a mind-set or innovation, from its inception to its broad-scale societal adoption, takes about the same amount of time as we human beings do to reach our adult prime of life. Life, at least for a radical new idea, does indeed begin at forty. What's especially interesting about this span of time is that the accelerating pace of technological evolution has not shortened the cycle. What took about forty years in the 1800s still takes about forty years today.

For example, the now nearly extinct electric filament lightbulb was invented in 1880 (one of the original applications of the new technology was a string of lights on a Christmas tree; it seemed wise to replace those dangerous candles). By the 1920s, large public spaces like ships were being wired and lit with tungsten bulbs. The first desktop computer was launched in 1965. By 2005, it was impossible to imagine contemporary life without one. The mobile phone was first demonstrated in 1973; today, it has surpassed the personal computer as the primary device for connecting to one another and the world. And the Internet itself? Its gestation began as a U.S. government research project in the early 1960s, but a version of the infrastructure so many of us cannot live without, in a form that would be vaguely recognizable to us today, was named "the Internet" in 1974. Forty years later its reach is still spreading by triple-digit percentages, and there's no area of modern life—from commerce to education to entertainment—that it hasn't touched and transformed.

You may be surprised to learn that 61 percent of the world's population is still not using the Internet. In effect, the net is still quite young. That's because the World Wide Web—our access to and interface with the Internet—was *invented* in 1990. Ordinary people didn't start getting online until the mid-90s. We're only about two decades into the web's adoption cycle. In other words, we still have much to learn about what it means to be ubiquitously and wholly connected to one another.

And yet, nearly 2.5 billion people around the world are online. And 6 billion people have a mobile device that connects them to others, and increasingly to the web. By any statistic, we are all more connected than ever before. And with connection comes knowledge and awareness. Knowledge and awareness that are set to increase exponentially as the next billion consumers come online.

Given this forty-year adoption curve, we might do well to ask ourselves: What was happening on the margins about forty years ago? What nascent trends and beliefs and technologies were born then and are now primed for global adoption, ready for their mainstream close-up?

Well, it's not a coincidence that the concept of, as well as the infrastructure for, cyberspace developed concurrently with the civil rights, women's liberation, gay pride, and environmental movements. It's not a coincidence that the movement for equal rights and the mobile phone emerged within just a few years of each other. The late '60s and early '70s were a fertile time for thinking about human liberation. A progressive and then-radical philosophy, fueled by a newly permissive and experimental environment on college campuses and by a sense of revolution against the established order and its unpopular politics (Vietnam anyone?), formed the beginning of a long-term movement.

The original cyber-thinkers were also unabashed hippies. That's because those with science and technology prowess, like avant-garde thinkers, tend to concentrate near top-tier universities. Northern California is home to numerous universities with strong engineering departments, and back in the late '60s and early '70s, as part of the back-to-the-land, do-it-yourself ethos, the locally created *Whole Earth Catalog* emerged as the go-to bible for everything from farming tools and beer-brewing supplies to components for building your own computer. This homemade computer movement spawned the personal computer industry—which, of course, began in the sunny and fertile microclimate now known as Silicon Valley. Meanwhile, Steve Jobs's own explorations of consciousness and LSD are to many as iconic as (and inseparable from) the groundbreaking company he founded. Empowerment and technology go hand in hand.

So it would seem that seeds of change planted forty years ago during the civil rights movement, nurtured through recessions and energy crises and globalization, have subsequently been fertilized by the rapid connection of billions to the Internet through personal computers and affordable mobile devices. The implications of ubiquitous connectivity are broad, but one of the most profound and widespread is the emergence of a "goodness imperative." It's more than an accelerating spread of global consciousness. It's a new global culture. Conscience Culture.

Jiminy Cricket, Buddha, Darwin, and You

> Yep, temptations. They're the wrong things that seem right at the time, but, uh…even though the right things may seem wrong sometimes, or sometimes the wrong things may be right at the wrong time, or visa versa. Understand?
>
> —Jiminy Cricket

Before we go further, a warning: Conscience Culture is the kind of topic your mother told you never to bring up in polite company—because it's impossible to talk about it without diving into subjects that can be rather polarizing, like religion, politics, and money—things I was taught to never discuss with strangers and dinner guests. But that's exactly what I'm going to do with you. As breezily as I can, so that no one gets upset and leaves the table.

In the animated film *Pinocchio*, Walt Disney famously depicted conscience as a charming and chirpy cricket. Very clever move. Conscience can feel heavy. Jiminy Cricket is probably the cutest and most unthreatening mascot for our inner sense of right and wrong that anyone has yet devised. That's Jiminy's definition of conscience, our inner sense of right and wrong. Double-click on conscience, and richer definitions emerge.

So let's put our first potentially polarizing bugbear briefly on the table—religion—because it's impossible to talk about right and wrong and not address it. All of the major world religions (and I'm referring to those faith traditions to which huge populations around the world adhere) in their own way put forth the idea that conscience is linked to divinity. For the believer, conscience connects one to a universal moral imperative dictated by a higher power, deity, or group of deities. From Buddhism to Hinduism to Islam to Judaism to Christianity, there is an established and fixed distinction between "good" and "evil." Yet it bears noting, especially for the skeptic or the atheist, that even within a religious context, conscience is designated as a *human* tool. Every major religion posits that each of us has our own conscience and that we should use it to ensure "right action" when making everyday decisions and choices.

For example, in Buddhism, conscience is a means of accessing compassion and empathy for all living things. According to the Catholic Church, conscience is an "act of the mind." In Islam, it's a "practice" that leads us to be accountable for how we live our lives. In other words, even within the dictates and moral strictures of religious belief, conscience is an expression of human free will. Indeed, conscience may be the only glue that links erstwhile conflicting theologies with atheism, because it is *human*.

Conscience is also social, and because of this, it's competitively advantageous for our species. Charles Darwin believed that human conscience evolved naturally, like every other aspect of our biological selves, as a mode of self-preservation. Conscience ensured the survival of the individual as well as of the family or community. Because the more social the species, the more interdependent each individual within that species is.

The actions of one impact the many. And thus, secularists and scientists argue, over the course of eons, conscience evolved to address the competitive interests of our species and therefore its survival.

Conscience Is Connection

When it comes to conscience, whether you take the resolutely secular view, the spiritual view, or some hybrid of the two, one thing is clear. Human beings are not born with a conscience. And if you lived your entire life in solitary confinement, you'd never develop one. Moreover, if you don't see anyone around you with a conscience, you'd lose whatever conscience you'd developed. Hannah Arendt, the celebrated philosopher and social psychologist, noted a loss of conscience on a mass scale in her observation and analysis of the psychology, both social and personal, of Nazi war criminals. Indeed, the systematic destruction of collective conscience is how some of our darkest human tragedies, mass atrocities and genocide, have come to pass. It's disturbing but true: conscience is not indestructible. Individual conscience can become sublimated by an onslaught of crushing bureaucracy and enforced adherence to rules that suppress the outward expression of right and wrong. Conscience needs community as much as community needs conscience.

That's because conscience emerges from connectedness and awareness. Your conscience and mine were formed directly in proportion to how connected we are, and to whom. Over the course of our development, we learn the implications of our actions. These implications are reinforced by parents, by teachers, in the playground, on the team, and at church or mosque or temple. The more they are reinforced, the stronger our conscience becomes.

Thus, my inner sense of right and wrong is shaped by my experience of being connected and experiencing the outcomes and effects of that connection. I am who I am because of you, and because of we. Our very interconnectedness is what keeps our conscience intact. We are one another's guardrails. The more connected and consequently the more interdependent we are, the more our actions impact others, and the more the reactions of others are reflected back onto us. We get back what we put out there. Whether you call it karma or "what comes around goes around," it's never been more true.

We are becoming increasingly aware of just how small our world really is. Look at the transformation of what were once considered externalities: the wide-ranging impacts of smoking, for example. We now know it isn't just smokers who suffer the consequences of their behavior, but others in their vicinity. We also know that the toxins in cigarettes eventually spread into aquatic ecosystems via discarded cigarette butts. Corporations (and governments) are no longer able to contain information about the impacts of using (or manufacturing) products or implementing policies. And unlike people in any previous era in society, we can now not only learn what's happening in faraway corners of the earth, we can usually even see and hear it in real time, online. So even if you don't see the conscience you seek in your next-door neighbors, you might find it expressed far away yet in the palm of your hand on your smartphone.

Here's an important distinction: it's not that a new generation are awakening as generous and selfless altruists. In fact, an emergent global conscience is merely a practical prerogative for human continuity in a world facing the consequences of unchecked population growth and limited natural resources. Given the threats we face and the problems that need solving, Darwin would say it's only natural. We're forming a global conscience because we *have* to. And because more people are sharing their own values and beliefs with others, conscience is reinforced further, and it grows. It's an upward spiral.

But it's not just about the real-time exchange of values. Conscience is also fortified by increasing knowledge. Your grandparents were less likely to care where their vegetables came from or how they were grown than you might, as long as they had some to put on the dinner table. The implications, both positive and negative, of mass agribusiness simply didn't matter to them, in no small part because they probably didn't know about them (or perhaps because mass agribusiness didn't yet exist, depending upon how old your grandparents are).

Earlier generations had different sensibilities about the ethics of child labor than most of us do today, in part because of economic realities that required most able-bodied human beings (even the very young) to work and in part because of differing notions of childhood itself. But concern for human well-being has long been part of our social nature, and in much of the world, as we've learned more about human development, the belief that childhood must be protected as a life phase dedicated to learning and growth has been enshrined in legal restrictions on child labor, and this idea continues to spread. It's a simple fact: common perception shifts as learning grows. Fast food was originally a miracle that liberated women from the kitchen so they could focus on careers, not a prime culprit in an epidemic of poor nutrition. Philanthropy was for railroad magnates and software billionaires, as was investing in promising business ideas—the rest of us had no place in these rarified domains. The ability to act on behalf of someone on the other side of the world was either the preserve of the very wealthy or the province of those with evangelical zeal. But knowledge advances our values and transforms our actions. Exponential increases in both the volume and accessibility of knowledge, as well as the continuous exchange of values, mean that more people feel compelled to mobilize to make a difference. We can act immediately on our smallest impulse or sense of injustice. The motivation isn't new; the empowerment is.

Win-Win

Youth groups travel halfway across the country in droves to rebuild towns devastated by superstorms and tornadoes—because it feels good. Young entrepreneurs put sweat equity into ride-sharing start-ups like Lyft or Sidecar that save fuel and change driving behavior by making carpooling into something exciting—because they want to make a difference. Clothing companies like TOMS Shoes attract young consumers by advocating the social and community benefits of their business model—because guilt-free, feel-good fashion is more fun. Menus in aspirational restaurants tout the local source of their vegetables—because we feel better about eating something that's connected to the earth. Bicycle lanes and a bike sharing program in charming Paris, sure, but in Noo Yawk City? The pedaling phenomenon—which has spread across more than thirty U.S. cities, from Anaheim to Tulsa to Washington, D.C.—has taken off so fast you'd think the United States invented the idea. As with any innovation, the initial executions of these developments may not be flawless, but they signal an intent to make positive social and environmental improvements through the basic infrastructure of daily life.

Alternative energy is no longer hippie talk; it's on every corporate board's agenda, because business requires a sustainable environment in which to flourish. And our 1880 tungsten lightbulb is finally at the end of its lifespan, because it turns out that saving energy with compact fluorescents also saves money—an easy win-win.

People everywhere are becoming more intuitively concerned about the implications of their individual actions. More of us than ever before are beginning to grasp the elusive truth that we really are all in this together. It's ubuntu.

The world is more connected than it's ever been. Individuals are more aware of the implications of their actions than ever before. Increasing numbers of us believe that even our climate is being directly affected by our actions. We debate whether new forms of harvesting gas like fracking are causing earthquakes. We wonder whether all of this wondrous connectivity has a dark side, the eradication of privacy. We are not the first generation to wonder whether the end is nigh, but we are the first to attempt to scientifically prove that our individual actions and everyday choices might have everything to do with it.

It often feels like technology and science are evolving faster than we can develop social norms and laws for protecting ourselves. Are we ready for nanotechnology, artificial intelligence, robot child care, or virtual doctors? Ready or not, they're coming, and we'll talk about them in a later chapter. Meanwhile, social behaviors on a mass scale are evolving faster than most organizations can.

Social enterprises are interesting harbingers of a new win-win model for business. Indeed, it seems as if the social enterprise is about to enter its heyday, such is the buzz around the concept. A social enterprise is a business that has as its primary purpose maximizing positive social impact while achieving financial goals. Contrary to popular belief, most social enterprises are for-profit businesses. The concept was born in the U.K. in the 1990s, and one frequently publicized statistic notes that in the U.K. alone there are in 2014 approximately 68,000 social enterprises that contribute more than £24 billion, or $40 billion, to its national economy.

Interestingly, because the precise legal definition of social enterprise or social venture has not been standardized, it's currently impossible to count the number of for-profit businesses globally that have, at their core, a social or environmental purpose. In a 2012 *Huffington Post* article, Ben Thornley, an expert in social entrepreneurship, estimated that the sector could soon generate revenues of $500 billion, or 3.5 percent of total U.S.

GDP, based on early results from the online registry the Great Social Enterprise Census. American business leaders are studying the social enterprise model, and the concept continues to get traction worldwide, in no small part because it advocates profitable problem solving.

The Conscience Economy is impacting the commercial world as much as it is the public sector. How businesses operate, how they communicate, and how they market and sell all fall under the microscope. Corporate reputation has never been more important, and communications transparency must be a given. But these are not enough. It's time to rethink our assumptions and our business models. There's no sector that won't be impacted. Just as the shift to digital technology and digitally enabled business models eventually disrupted every category of business, the prerogatives of an emergent Conscience Economy will shake up—and revitalize—business as a whole. Ethical production and sustainable sourcing are the tip of an iceberg of Conscience Economy concerns. As it becomes ever more possible (and mandatory) to collect information from every transaction, new dilemmas arise. Personal data management and consumer privacy are perhaps the most critical future differentiator as more and more aspects of daily life move online and leave a data footprint, from financial transactions to health (an issue we will explore in a later chapter).

There's plenty of work to do. But what an opportunity!

Global connectedness. Increasing awareness of our interdependence. Personal empowerment. A nagging sense that we have urgent problems to solve in order for humanity to thrive. A forty-year gestation period from the progressive early '70s to today. These are the dimensions of increasing consciousness that have converged to create the conditions for a mass shift in mainstream mind-set and values. And this shift is impacting your customers, your electorate, your family, your community, and even your own personal choices.

Imagine the possibilities not only for your enterprise, but for your own satisfaction and personal well-being, not to mention that of your employees, partners, and customers, once you harness the power of the Conscience Economy. Humans are essentially social. We need to be a part of something bigger than ourselves in order to truly self-actualize. Now more than ever, no matter your livelihood or lifestyle, like our Young Turk you *can* do well and do good. The new chapter has only just begun.

Get Ready

The world is moving rapidly from being *conscious* to acting with *conscience*. What about your business?

To thrive in the Conscience Economy, every business will need to adapt and transform what it offers, how it produces, how it operates, how it sells, and how it engages others. Transformation is a muscle. It strengthens with use, it atrophies with neglect. Businesses that not only survive but *thrive* in the Conscience Economy will consider transformation—at both the corporate and individual level—a core competency.

The first step: ensuring that you and your business culture are ready to change. It all starts with a company-wide mind-set of openness. Is your business—as a business—broadly conscious of the social, technological, cultural, and environmental shifts that will impact future success? Does your business currently embody a shared conscience, a collective and intuitive sense of what constitutes doing the right thing, not only for the bottom line but for the wider world? You need to assess where your business stands in terms of its readiness and motivation to change for good.

The process of transforming—whether self, or group, or business, or nation—is a process of conversation. A frank, look-in-the-mirror, permission-to-speak-the-truth multidirectional conversation. I'm not suggesting all talk and no action. But there will be no action *without* talk. Dialogue creates an environment of openness, which leads to experimentation and learning, which informs further dialogue, which leads to further experimentation and learning and application, and faster than we think, we've achieved progress. That sounds like therapy, you're thinking. Yup. It's also like Olympic team coaching, feature film directing, and raising a family.

Start the conversation that will prepare your business for success in the Conscience Economy. It's not hard. You just do it. Start asking questions, ideally from the top, because that's where the tone is set.

Some questions to consider, as part of formal or informal conscience conversations:

- Is your organizational culture more internally or externally focused?
- Does your organization have a track record of successfully adapting to external forces of change?

- Do you look outside your industry for clues, ideas, and inspiration? Or do you only see relevance in your direct competitive set?
- Is there a sense of urgency to try doing things differently? How does your organization treat risk taking and failure?
- Is your organization aggressively forward looking, firmly rooted in the urgencies of the present, or riding high on its past successes?
- Is the increasing importance of balancing positive environmental and social impact with profit on the company's radar screen? Do you consign it to a CSR department or embed it in everyone's daily awareness?

By just asking the questions—with your board, with your colleagues, with your team, with your boss, and even with your partners and customers—you automatically introduce the *possibility* for transformation and invite participation in the collective process of advancing your business. There are no right answers to the questions above. They are catalysts. They shift your business's mind-set. By doing so, you begin to nurture your organization's own nascent conscience.

Once people recognize the possibilities for doing well by doing good, emotional motivations—the personal satisfaction of having meaningful work, the thrill of becoming part of a new and better world—take over, driving passion and momentum throughout the enterprise. And you can channel that momentum into a series of company-wide initiatives that simultaneously engage employees emotionally and optimize business operations to adapt to the emerging business environment. Continual transformation that's fueled by a sense of higher purpose is more likely to take hold.

Ultimately, the unstoppable rise of the Conscience Economy is a phenomenon of mass enlightened self-interest. More than ever, more of us want to do more good, because it's good for us. Consciousness has led to conscientiousness. Awareness is morphing into action, because now we are living with the urgency of a set of converging circumstances we can no longer ignore. Everything is on the line. We've gotten a big wake-up call.

2

The Big Wake-Up Call

L ast summer, I went to visit my parents in my home state of New Jersey. Earlier in the year, the state's coastal areas had been ravaged by Hurricane Sandy, a class 2 "superstorm" that inflicted approximately $68 billion in damage. Thousands of homes and businesses had been destroyed on the legendary Jersey Shore, which has an economy largely dependent on beach tourism. Months later, the state was beginning to rebuild.

I wanted to see how the reconstruction was getting along. We drove through town to the bridge that crosses a small river onto the barrier beach of Sea Bright, one of many towns that was battered by waves during the hurricane. Many homes and businesses in the town were still boarded up, and some beachfront buildings I'd known from childhood had been washed out to sea. They were simply gone.

Anyway, on the bridge that leads from the mainland onto the barrier beach, traffic slowed into a jam. My father explained why. "The fire department is taking up a collection to support the local reconstruction of the beaches." I looked at the volunteers in their Day-Glo vests, at the well-intentioned donating by each and every driver. I couldn't help but notice that each and every driver happened to be driving a gas-guzzling SUV.

Sure, I admit, there's no evidence that driving an SUV causes a hurricane. And it is no one's fault that the natural disaster happened. This is why the insurance industry calls such catastrophic events "acts of God." I readily admit to my own history of dinner-table skepticism about the notion that human involvement is the prime cause of dramatic climate change, but it must be said that there *is* increasing evidence that fossil fuel consumption is contributing to global warming, which contributes to rising sea levels, which will ultimately, and sooner than anyone wants to admit, eradicate the beach that these well-intentioned gas-guzzling drivers are donating their spare dollar bills in order to save.

So there's a measure of cause and effect, even if it's minute.

It's interesting that we can so effortlessly ignore how our individual choices contribute even in small ways to what is literally in front of our eyes—in this instance, a disappearing and economically valuable coastline. But there's growing awareness that there's something going on with our climate that poses a major threat to our lives. The White House has even put a dollar figure on the cost of the problem, claiming that climate change cost the U.S. economy $100 billion in 2012, the nation's warmest year on record.

I'm reminded of a conversation I had with Todd, a very articulate young writer and carpenter from Maine who's currently working in a bicycle shop in Barcelona, where, I add with both admiration and the tiniest of eye rolls, the young bearded entrepreneurs are building bicycles out of sustainably sourced bamboo while brewing artisanal organic coffee. We got to talking about where he thinks things are heading. "The question," he said, when I told him what I was writing about, "is one of agency. Can each of us really impact the larger system? Do we have agency?" And this, what almost sounded like cynicism, from an extremely thoughtful member of the millennial generation who, regardless of his sense that he may or may not impact the future, still chooses to live and work in a highly localized, environmentally sensible, socially progressive way. His question of agency interests me, because evidence suggests that more and more people choose to act as if they can and will impact the system.

Continuous transformation is the world's underlying scheme. Yet given the chance, we usually turn away from it, often because we feel that there's nothing we can do about it.

That is, until we've reached a moment full of evidence from which we can't turn away any longer. It's like an alcoholic reaching the proverbial rock bottom. And we've reached that moment *now*. All human endeavor and technological progress, since we first stood on two feet and threw a rock to defend ourselves or acquire dinner, has led to a future-defining moment in our evolution—a singular conflux of irreversible social progress and technological innovation. It's unlike any moment humanity has faced before, a big wake-up call that's upending our priorities. After forty years of moving from the margin to the mainstream, this wake-up call is the ultimate catalyst of the Conscience Economy.

The Great Conflux

Why did a Conscience Economy not rise out of the smoking ashes of a broken world in 1948? After all, people across the planet had experienced or seen broadcast images of unspeakable cruelty, crumbling nations, and broken enterprise. They'd united for common cause and won. Or what about the 1960s, a time of so much hope and tumult and liberation? Or the 1990s, with its recession-era soul-searching in the wake of a decade of greed, and the birth of the suddenly browsable and thus easily accessed web? What's so different now? Why is *now* the moment?

Of course, previous eras of societal rebuilding and broad economic reconfiguration have indeed contributed to the foundations for the current mass movement for good. But this moment, as I am committing these words to the screen and you are reading them, bears hallmarks that are both ominous and hopeful in equal measure. What used to be science fiction has become (as is so often the case with the sci-fi genre) simply science. Or more accurately, simply headline news.

To state the obvious, what's radically different today is not one thing, but many, in concert. The size and growth rate of Earth's population. The steady (and successful) march of human rights movements across the planet. The change in environmental conditions. But the biggest difference of all, the one that ultimately gives rise to the Conscience Economy, is technology. Particularly connected technology. It's both the catalyst and the content of civilization's big wake-up call. In the right hands, it informs and empowers us. In the wrong hands, it endangers us.

We are currently living through what I call a major *conflux*. A coming together of various driving forces that are leading us toward a tipping point of significant, possibly cataclysmic change. In no particular order, let's whizz through some of the most significant change drivers that have moved from the margins into mass consciousness.

A Fragile Environment

Care for the environment has moved from a fringe priority to the refrain of indignant second graders when they see a grown-up trying to chuck a plastic bottle into the trash. "Don't throw that away. It's bad for the environment." Steadily increasing awareness of the fragility of our natural ecosystem, and our role in sustaining it, have been augmented by a series of natural events that, whether caused by humanity or not, have raised huge questions about the future. Depleted reservoirs and dry riverbeds, superstorms, dramatic climate swings, shrinking glaciers, rising sea levels: sustainability is no longer the province of left-wing environmentalists.

Environmental advocacy has been professionalized and standardized, and as a notion, it's as ubiquitous as freedom itself. It's even exploited. Supermarket shelves are laden with expensive "green" products. Hotels ask us to "save water" (read: save laundry costs). In cities like San Francisco plastic bags are outlawed. And here's the thing: whether a recent spate of freak weather was caused by us or not, we no longer talk about it as freak weather. While we line up at the checkout counter stocking up on water and batteries as a threatening superstorm rolls up the coast or a freak blizzard heads our way, we are starting to question our role in the changing climate. Whether provable or not, the notion that we are changing the nature of the universe's only known inhabitable planet is on our minds. Because it's probably true.

Scarce Resources

Natural capital is not unlimited. Depending upon the news cycle, the hot button impending shortage can be energy, it can be food, it can be water, it can be copper. What we know is that we have not yet found a way to make our essential resources for living and working and thriving self-sustainable. Meanwhile, distribution is usually our biggest challenge today. It's not that this is new news. It's that resource scarcity is affecting increasing numbers of people who'd previously believed they'd advanced beyond it, who believed they lived with expendable abundance. Consider the citizens of the Golden State of California, with their droughts, wildfires, and brownouts. Resource scarcity is one of the primary sources (if not *the* primary source) of geopolitical conflict. And not just far away. Even if it ultimately helps heat our homes, no one wants fracking in his backyard. Every business—like every person—relies on natural resources in order to exist.

Genetic Engineering

Humans have always tinkered with genetics. Gigi, my parents' designed-to-be-adorable Maltese terrier, is a lovable, cuddly product of advanced genetic engineering from four hundred years ago. But now that we've actually decoded the genome, ostensibly making the foundations of life itself into a kit of parts that can be remixed and reassembled, the cuddliness of gene play has vaporized. Food farming was the first battleground. Across Europe, the wholesale rejection of genetically modified crops is inscribed in law. This is not, as you might think, because tradition-bound Europeans are creeped out by the thought of eating a tomato created in a laboratory. It's because no one knows the consequences of the uncontrollable and inevitable interaction between genetically modified crops and an unmodified ecosystem. But it's already too late.

For the record, I'm no genetic Luddite; indeed, the mass movement for good—from improving food supply stability to bolstering nutrition and disease defense to efficient data storage and identity management—will be well served by innovation that's rooted in tinkering with the genome. But what's next on this road? Human cloning is inevitable, perhaps initially in the name of disease treatment and organ replacement; creating partially human beings would be a logical next step. And it doesn't matter if we ban human cloning on the grounds of mass moral outrage. The cat's out of the bag. If there's market demand for it, or some kind of humanitarian argument in defense of cloning emerges, why wouldn't someone, somewhere, make it happen? As with the invention of weapons of mass destruction, we can't simply erase human developments and discoveries, no matter how morally repugnant they may seem. If we can crack the genome, we can hack the genome. After all, it's code like any other. Look up biohacking. It's here.

Networked Warfare

Flashpoints of deadly conflict continue to erupt in fought-over geographies and cities. But over the last three decades, we've seen wars increasingly waged through networks of terrorist cells operating in places far from the original source of tension. Fatal attacks on civilians in global cities in effect transport the front lines of battle into the global marketplace. So far, this is a losing strategy, but an unintended consequence of networked warfare is that wars of ideas and values (for example, fundamentalist Islam versus "the West") are omnipresent, and more of us are more aware than ever of how difficult it is to be a girl in Afghanistan.

At the same time, networked war is effective, and oddly less violent than its prior form. Year by year, though conflicts continue, fewer people are dying in wars than ever before. Harvard psychologist Steven Pinker's research for his book *The Better Angels of Our Nature: Why Violence Has Declined* shows a steady decrease in the percentage of people killed in conflict. His findings are substantiated by statistics analyzed by other experts, including Andrew Mack, former head of strategic planning for Kofi Annan at the United Nations. The facts run counter to our gut feeling—because of the increase in violence we *see* online and in the news. It may feel more horrifying, because violence is more public—in real time—when it happens. The point is, we all feel closer to the implications of conflict, and not only because we have to take our shoes off at airport security or put off that beach holiday in Beirut for another season. When radical Islamists in any part of the world start acting up, we feel a tiny bit nervous on the London Underground. We're simply closer to the front lines, everywhere. Which is why we all feel it's our right to weigh in on the issues. But our awareness of violence could be the very reason that, statistically, it's in year-on-year decline. Though it must be said: one nuclear weapon could still change everything.

Health-Care Volatility

Here lies a mess of anomalies. More of humanity is healthier than ever before, and life expectancy is steadily increasing in much of the world. But simultaneously, there is a broad sense that health care is in crisis. It is regularly reported that within our lifetime we may experience a meltdown of antibiotic effectiveness, thanks to their overuse. The threat of a global pandemic of untreatable and fatal avian flu pops up in the headlines regularly. An obesity "epidemic" is growing across the U.S. and the U.K., fueled in part by increasing poverty and the comforts of highly processed (shareholder-return-feeding) fast food—and yet obesity-related disease in the U.S. alone costs the public coffers upward of $117 billion annually. In those countries that provide health care, social health-care systems are overstretched. In those that don't, heated debates rage over whether to build one or not. Broad arguments are being expressed in the public sphere. Is health an individual's responsibility, when our wellness depends upon broader social infrastructure? Meanwhile, people are living longer and will consequently need more care. Who is accountable? Must government always be the answer?

Artificial Intelligence

At the time of this writing, the capabilities of artificial intelligence are limited, and generally delightful. Indeed, we long for more of it. Who among us doesn't love when our music stream seems to pick the exact right song for us? And who wouldn't prefer a more personal, intelligent autocorrect on her smartphone? We are regularly reassured that it's unlikely engineers can create a computer that is smarter than a human being. At least not next quarter. Such a relief.

In the meantime, artificial intelligence is also used in search engines to help you find what you're seeking. How nice. It's used to scan your life and discover patterns in your behavior and your communication but not—as far as I know, and I've been involved in plenty of decisions about data mining for marketing purposes—on *your* behalf as a customer. As more information and even service jobs become automated, we won't be able to live without highly sophisticated artificial intelligence; we'll invest more and more in it, and its IQ will increase.

Google director of engineering Ray Kurzweil and mathematician Vernor Vinge have even forecast the future occurrence of what Kurzweil refers to as the singularity, a hypothetical moment in time when global computing power will be able to outthink humanity. The date? Sometime between 2017 and 2045. At least that's not tomorrow. Wait—2017? So are we on our way to assembling the dystopic Skynet of the blockbuster Terminator movies? The Scarlett Johansson–voiced titular object of affection in Spike Jonze's *Her*? It doesn't bear thinking about. Or does it? Maybe I'll just get back to my amazing Spotify playlist.

Evaporation of Privacy

Ubiquitous digital connectedness is a way of life and even perceived by many of us as a human right. But what about privacy? That convenient free Wi-Fi at the airport? Forget all the hoo-ha about the NSA spying on people in Germany—even the fairness-loving Canadians were recently exposed for using airport Wi-Fi to siphon information out of travelers' smartphones and laptops.

It would be nice if privacy, like vinyl records, bicycles, and barbershops, made a comeback with the next generation. But right now, they can't even understand what it once was. As everything we do becomes digitally and contextually enabled, we leave a footprint behind us, a permanent footprint indelibly etched into searchable big data. Where do all these footprints lead?

I mentioned my concern about the evaporation of privacy to a young colleague a few months ago. Her response was fascinating, and not atypical of her cohort. "I don't really mind," she said, "because I never do anything illegal." This was a highly thoughtful young woman, well-educated, successful, progressive. But the blind spot in her logic is concerning, and spoke volumes about a new generation that accepts that all they do is trackable, trading privacy in the interest of convenience. But what if she lived in a place where it were illegal for her to have sex before marriage? She might feel differently about her privacy.

My young colleague's response to my question may seem to support the broadly held view among market researchers that "millennials don't care about privacy." But a closer inspection of their values reveals a more complex picture. Members of the new generation are willing—even eager—to have their needs and behaviors revealed to the world, as long as they benefit from the exchange. But the next generation is among the most engaged in the increase in civil liberties, as evidenced by the high percentage of support for same-sex marriage. Meanwhile, they are among the most outraged when they learn that their civil liberties have been impinged upon. NSA whistle-blower Edward Snowden, who as of this writing is still on the lam—ironically, in Moscow—exemplifies millennial values in action.

Total connectivity is indeed convenient, increasingly essential, and arguably addictive. Opting out is difficult. Peer-to-peer networks don't yet offer sufficient coverage. And so we choose to give up our privacy every day. But it's an uneasy deal. Should our personal information be used against us the tide may turn, leading to a wholesale rejection of traditional networks in favor of here today, gone tomorrow peer-to-peer solutions. Snapchat could be a harbinger of an embrace of personal privacy. But an older generation's mistrust of the system might be the catalyst needed to lead the charge if we want to avert a systemic breach of personal privacy. It's in business's (and everyone's) best interests to maintain identity management codes of conduct that put the human, and not the corporation, first.

Nanotechnology

Moore's Law—which forecasts the consistent miniaturization of computing power—has held relatively steady for more than forty years. How much smaller (read: invisible) can technology get? Circuitry can already be built at the molecular scale. We're blurring the boundaries between nature and technology. Some would argue that those boundaries have already dissolved. When technology—particularly sensor technology— can be embedded in everything and everyone, what type of world will we have created? A techno-paradise of interconnected data feeds? An overdependence on technological connectivity such that when something breaks or is hacked, we're unable to function? And when it's embedded in us, will we still be human? Or will we be superhuman?

The Sensor Revolution

Sensors are the basis of the next massive wave of innovation. But sensors are not new—their connectedness is. As I've often said in my keynote speeches about the future of smartphones, the lens is not just for taking pictures. It's an eye that sees where you are, who you are with, the weather, the light levels, the traffic. And the microphone doesn't just transport your voice. It's an ear that can sense all aural information about your context.

But these were just the beginning. Next came GPS, which knows and broadcasts our location. Just as our own five senses (or six, depending upon what you believe) help us understand and navigate our world, sensors will help businesses and governments understand and navigate us. Because we are about to inhabit an everyday environment of proliferating and interconnected sensors. They will fill our homes, sit in our pockets, wrap around our wrists, be embedded in our shoes, pepper the inside and outside of our cars. Indeed, the under-construction Internet of Things is largely being built out of them. They open up almost unimaginable possibilities for new types of contextual experiences, both wondrous and dark. Because it means that everything you do is trackable and knowable. Including your personal biology.

The Quantified Self

Today, you choose your mobile device because its platform supports your favorite apps, because it has a good camera, because it integrates effortlessly with your other tech gear. But in the very near future, we will be choosing our mobile device because it's the one that helps us stay healthier and live longer. Mobiles will monitor and help us improve our biological condition. Today's tech R&D agendas, hiring briefs, and acquisition and patent portfolios point clearly to the quantified self as a major source of future innovation.

Wearables like Nike's FuelBand or Jawbone's UP24 already record and upload information that indicates our fitness levels and more into the cloud, and encourage us to exercise more or more effectively across multiple devices. These are benign and even highly appealing use cases of sensor technology.

Meanwhile, economic strain on health providers will force many aspects of the health-care system to be digitized, mobilized, and virtualized. For example, today many diagnostic detection processes are chemical—in other words, a sample of your pee or your blood needs to have a chemical additive in order to identify markers of a particular condition. But increasingly, detection systems are being developed that are optical. These innovations will decrease the reliance on—and cost of—physical labs, and make accurate virtual diagnosis possible. Already there are virtual diagnosis technologies in development for optically identifiable diseases like melanoma. In the future, they'll be deployed to monitor markers like blood sugar levels.

But these remarkable technologies are by their nature connected. And they'll detect things we may not want shared. The quantified self will mean that we are all utterly naked. Every heartbeat will be recorded and saved in the cloud. When and where we ate, drank, and even, according to an investor in this technology whom I recently spoke with, when and where we last orgasmed. (By detecting highly specific heart-rate patterns and circulatory fluctuations, in case you're curious.)

You can go ahead and chuckle at that, unless you live in a place where the restrictions of Ramadan are strictly enforced. The dilemmas of the quantified self are serious. What if, for example, a mobile sensor detected your probability of developing a particular cancer. Could that probability be characterized as a pre-existing condition? At the time of this writing, legally, according to HIPAA laws in the United States, a patient cannot be denied health-care coverage due to a preexisting condition. But if a patient doesn't disclose what they know about their health, they will be denied coverage, which demonstrates that insurance companies do have a right to know something. How much? And what about in the rest of the world? Today's laws and ethical norms—not to mention health-care and insurance business models—weren't developed in the context of such detailed biometric information and the probabilities that information depicts, which will soon be readily available.

Citizen Amateurs

The easy express-and-broadcast capabilities of the web—and particularly its mobile accessibility—has created a wave of amateurization across every discipline. On the surface of things, this is wondrous and liberating. But it has a dark side, too.

Let's look at journalism, which has been profoundly affected by this trend. Newspapers, in their struggle for a sustainable business model now that the classifieds business is long dead, can barely support proper investigative journalism anymore. The discipline has been replaced by a constant stream of tweets, pictures, personal opinions, reasonably informed blogs, YouTube videos, and other "democratically" sourced content—remixed by the reader on Flipboard or the personalized aggregator of his choice. Again, on the surface, this seems benign. Everyone gets a voice. What's wrong with that?

On the other hand, investigative journalism is a skill that requires fine-tuning over the years. Investigative journalism—which the good old newspapers like *The Philadelphia Inquirer* were built upon and lauded for—is, according to its former editor Robert Rosenthal, who's now the executive director of a Bay Area nonprofit called the Center for Investigative Reporting (CIR), "the lifeblood of democracy." It's about getting to the tough story, getting behind the walls and under the floors, uncovering what's invisible, and shining fresh light on what's often dark. Proper and professional journalism plays a crucial role in a free society, which is why freedom of the press is sacred in cultures that value personal liberty. Even if well-intentioned, "most amateurs," CIR's Rosenthal told me over coffee in his appropriately noir-ish windowless office, "don't have the training, the reporting skills to really investigate."

For a new generation, the voices and images of amateurs are perceived as having equal validity to those of the professionals. But generally, the amateurs only share what's right in front of them or what's in their minds. There's been much celebration (outside of the traditional media brands, that is) of the "democratization" of journalism. So here's a seemingly disconnected but relevant question: Would you prefer your kids' health in the hands of "citizen health providers" or a trained pediatrician?

Career Transience

The days of the corporate insider rising to the top may well be numbered, because in the foreseeable future, a talented stable of insiders will be an endangered species. The next generation expects no loyalty from employers, and will likely work not only for multiple employers but through multiple careers in their working life. If they believe they can even get work. Years of mass unemployment in markets like Spain have left a generation feeling cynical about corporate participation, reliant on social services for their very existence, yet highly informed, as many have spent their workless time educating themselves.

The uncertainty that millennials face has given birth to deeply felt motivations that stand in stark contrast to the type of employee motivations that drove business growth for the past few decades. Although many are self-directed and ambitious, they are also used to being financially reliant on others (parents, friends, the government). They will work for you, if you prove to them what's in it for them. It's unlikely that the most talented will stick around if they spot a new opportunity. Not only because their attention spans are shorter (which is true, and a factor), but because they don't place their trust in the stability of employment. They trust themselves.

One of the offshoots of constant instability and the realization among young people that they are unlikely to have continuous, stable, and lucrative employment is a desire to find work that's meaningful. Sherilyn Shackell, an executive recruiter and marketing educator in London, recently told me that she thinks that meaningful organizations will be "the next talent drain." When I asked her what she meant by this, she said, "A few years ago, everyone wanted to join a tech start-up. Today, I'm seeing people compete even harder for less-lucrative roles but in socially impactful organizations. They want to feel like all the time they're spending is doing something good for someone else. Work is life, and they want life to be meaningful."

How-ism

People also look for meaning in the things that they buy, not just how they spend their time. And because of the easy availability of information, people are increasingly coming to understand that every product made or grown is not only comprised of its materiality, but of processes. How and where a product or service or foodstuff was produced matters more to people than ever before, because it's on the radar screen.

A proliferation of certifications and labels like free range, cruelty free, slavery free, organic, conflict-free, Rainforest Alliance Certified, Fair Trade Certified, and more signify the increasing attention given to the way a product or food was produced. Although such signifiers began as a means of addressing the demands of a niche segment of the population, the cohort choosing products based upon these certifications is rapidly growing and increasingly loyal. Consumers prefer to buy from companies they trust, and people-friendly, healthy, and safe production processes are the surest sign of trustworthiness. Meanwhile, concepts like "carbon footprints" and "food miles" have become mainstream standards for discussing and improving the social and ecological impact of business. Even the political biases and donations of corporate executives factor into the should-I-buy-it equation.

Neo-Anticapitalism

A new generation's wholesale rejection of the basic principles of capitalism as we know it looms as a very real possibility. Just ask your kids what they think. For example, the Occupy movement is more than a fringe group that resents executive success. It is the most vocal and visible expression of a broad dissatisfaction with an all-too-real and growing wealth gap between the top and the bottom segments of society.

We can make all the arguments we want about the motivating power of an unregulated free market. We can explain why unregulated compensation for top talent is utterly fair as one of the free market's core ingredients. I myself am uncomfortable with the whole notion of "equality" as an aspiration when it comes to compensation, or anything other than human civil rights. Fairness, however, is a different story. Even so, make no mistake: the argument for the performance-motivating power of unfettered financial compensation won't be heard, because mass resentment is real, and it's growing. Making it onto the presidential agenda in the form of the income inequality debate has given this dissatisfaction the stamp of legitimacy.

Though many might welcome it, it's unlikely we'll experience the drama of a French Revolution–style class upheaval. No, the new guillotines will have gentler blades, but the cuts could be just as fatal. Perhaps it will take the form of a gradual wind-down of consumer spending (after all, they'll have less money) in favor of an increase in sharing and self-producing. To the extent that they can, many are already creating new systems of self-sufficiency that they perceive to be more just and fair. The good news is, there will be global businesses that will thrive by helping the dissatisfied masses do just this.

Alternative Currencies

One response to the global financial system is the establishment of alternative currency. Bitcoin is just the beginning. Actually, some say that shopper loyalty points and frequent flier miles were the original alternative currencies. No matter. The point is that the currencies we all know and use have a very different meaning to a new generation who take hacking, making, and manipulating data for granted. After all, money is data too. The noise level around the very utility of money itself is rising, as is, I should mention, questions about the utility of capitalism itself. To many readers, this will sound extreme, and extremist. Don't close the book. Because who would have thought that *The Matrix*-style peer-to-peer currency created by a shadowy network of hackers would have been discussed seriously by the global elite at Davos? That scenario is already in the public record.

New Crimes

Surprising as it may seem, physical crime as a whole is going down dramatically in major cities around the world. But new forms of cyber crime are on the rise, both in actuality and in the public mind. As we become ever more dependent on connected data, the value of that data grows higher and more worthy of theft. Identity theft is expensive. Intellectual property theft is business threatening. Holding entire communities or businesses hostage to a hacked energy grid, hijacking driverless transport, holding up supply-and-demand chains by intercepting data flows—these and more are potential scenarios for organized crime syndicates to siphon value out of a virtualized financial network. Data encryption remains a vital domain for robust and continuous innovation.

The Crossroads

Each one of these change drivers, when considered on its own, is significant. But merged together, they form a whole greater than the sum of its parts. If we were to simply let things run their course, without addressing how we, as an interdependent community of human beings, want our world, our lives, and our businesses to be for our children and our successors, things might not turn out to be so life enhancing for all.

It's not hard to imagine how it could all go. Imagine a world without individual privacy, where everything about us—our thoughts, expressions, and biology—is connected and knowable by friends and enemies alike, creating new healthy haves and healthless have-nots as well as new forms of untraceable and total identity theft and trade. A world where real-world currencies compete with decentralized forms of exchange that are more appealing to a generation with less opportunity to earn. Where climate change threatens to put our greatest financial centers literally underwater, not to mention scores of human lives, while simultaneously and ironically water shortages cause uprisings of conflict that play out far beyond their geographic place of origin. Where your intellectual property and your talent are impossible to protect from the reaching grasp of your competition. Imagine a world where an increasingly strained health-care system results in the slowdown of life expectancy gains and puts ever greater pressure on public coffers. Where robots raise and teach our kids, if they haven't yet taken our jobs or started governing us. Where masses of frustrated and connected citizens demand greater regulation of big business from their governments even as those governments are fragmenting into smaller and smaller communities of interest. Where there are imposed limits on compensation as well as business growth. Where people stop using banks or participating in broader economic value creation but instead make and trade peer to peer. Imagine a world where mob opinion takes over from fact and truth. The list could go on. It's not sci-fi. It's possible.

However, an alternative and happier future is far more likely, because it too is possible. More people are more aware of the impact that our actions—and particularly the actions of large and powerful organizations—have on human life and continuity. A digitally empowered society will decide how we want all this to play out. We know it wouldn't be sensible to simply let our humanity and our planet go. Because we're social by nature, humans have a tendency, in the end, to make life better for one another, not worse. We've never had a better opportunity to do just that on a mass scale than we do right now. And thanks to the unstoppable conflux, it's never been more urgent.

As individuals, we may be tempted to just let things run their course. It's natural to not want to face what's right in front of us. But businesses—and business leaders—cannot afford to turn away from the conflux and assume that things will continue as usual. The wisest and most effective competitive and growth strategies will engage directly in all or most of the discussed change drivers. They are already impacting your business whether you have begun to acknowledge it or not. The co-founder and former editor of *Wired* magazine, Louis Rossetto, used to keep a Post-it note on his computer at all times. It said, "deal with change before change deals with you."

So what's a business to do?

Adapting to change is hard. It takes strong motivation to commit to making operational and cultural adjustments both great and small. The drive to overcome inertia and make the necessary changes can be sparked by embedding future-friendly awareness across the organization. Everyone needs a regular wake-up call. By personally confronting the changes that our businesses, and their functions, are facing, we absorb these changes more deeply, and they start to inform the strategic and operational decisions we make regularly. It's not enough to simply be told. We need to see where we're going ourselves. The firsthand experience of envisioning our own future is simply more catalytic than reading it in a memo or report.

It's a wise habit for all leaders to be personally conversant in at least the basics of techno-social and behavioral foresight. Indeed, in a world that's shifting so quickly, a bit of insight and foresight needs to be part of every manager's job. Like feeling the effect of weather conditions on the road on which we're driving, we need to personally engage the sometimes almost invisible, sometimes seemingly faraway forces that are in fact impacting what we do in the here and now.

I've heard the push backs. "But we need to address declining sales today. We don't have the luxury of time for star-gazing or intellectual stuff," thinks the prototypical and hyper-focused head of sales. "This is why we have a strategy department, and why they hire a consultancy. I don't have time to think about anything but my team. When we get a break, maybe we can talk about the future." These are understandable sentiments. Indeed, the real-time demands of the present moment can make talking about the future seem like a luxury. But everything I have described in the list of driving forces above is happening now. We're all on the trajectory. And there are knowledge gaps to fill, as quickly as possible. We all need to know the world in which we're operating. Most of us know and operate in our own vision of the world, and in our own business's vision of the world. It's surprisingly easy for management to become myopic, even in (and in some ways, especially in) the technology sector. Even seemingly unstoppable tech giants are vulnerable to imminent irrelevance. Remember when the Internet meant AOL?

Knowledge is power. Foresight is superpower. And the good news is, it's also very easy to expand and extend your own—and your team's—scope of vision, and harness the superpower of foresight in everyday decisions. And what's more, it's fascinating and engaging. It sparks conversations, enlivens meetings, provokes new solutions. It's not a challenging muscle to develop. But it is a different muscle than the one most leaders use every day. You simply need to build your own change-driver telescope.

Build Your Telescope

As a brand strategist and business innovation guy, it has long been my job to peer into the near future and get a bead on what's coming next. Some called this skill "understanding emergence." And I'll tell you something: it's easy, once you give yourself the creative permission to do it. The first step is acknowledging that it's an essential part of your job.

To see what's emerging we simply do this: synthesize our own observations with our own finely honed intuition. We look at what's around us, every day, with an open mind, without assumptions. What are people doing in their cars, on the bus, at the coffee shop? We look for aspects of everyday life and media that somehow stand out—fast-spreading social media memes, news articles, shops, consumer products, new kinds of services—that stand out. And we look for patterns. Clusters of similar circumstances, sentiments, or entities. When we spot something that is difficult or unlikely, or doesn't follow a traditional business logic but begins to unfold anyway, it's a sign that we should take notice.

The "telescope" I use includes a range of activities. I don't just read the media, I scan it regularly for new phenomena and emergent popular ideas. I also consult oracles—my sexy description of talking to experts and thought leaders about what they think and see. Over the years, as these activities have become a habit, I've learned to recognize patterns in behavior and ideas, just as you will. There are "early warning signs" when a new trend or phenomenon is taking hold. Often, a trend has an epicenter, and I assess whether the trend is exportable to new contexts and cultures or business categories.

The web makes this easy to access, though potentially overwhelming. From TED Talks to *Wired* online to a proliferation of blogs, there's so much out there. So start with the change drivers listed in this chapter. Choose a few—make sure there's at least one that excites you and at least one that really bothers you—and spend a few minutes discovering more about them online. *Do not have your assistant do this for you.* Your own discovery is what will embed foresight into your managerial thinking. Save some bookmarks in your browser. Keep a small list in your notebook. The object: make surveying emergent change drivers as much a habit as checking the share prices.

There are four key principles to put in play as you build and use your telescope.

1. ***Self-source it.*** You do the discovering. Reading a deck of slides that someone else put together for you just doesn't work. You'll quickly forget—if you read them at all. You and your team have to identify emerging change drivers yourselves. In other words, don't just outsource your future vision to the innovation department. It's most effective to have a *felt* experience of the possibilities of change.

2. ***Make it relevant.*** It's wise to start by identifying change drivers from outside your business space; you must establish their relevance— whether direct or indirect—to your business ecosystem. Next, you nail the relevance link. *Briefly* verbalize why this matters for your business. Keep it simple. Just two things. How is this change driver— or better yet, try a mash-up of several change drivers—good for your business, and how is it bad for your business?

3. ***Invite your team to participate.*** Get everyone on your team thinking about change drivers on a regular basis. Have each team member "own" a particular change driver, assign a monthly wake-up call champion, or let it happen organically. Incentivize people to come up with the most insightful and relevant observations. Use the context

of change drivers in creative brainstorms, even those about internal processes and operational challenges.

4. ***Build it into everyday work***. Begin every meeting—and I'm not using the word "every" lightly—from the outside in. Put a "wake-up call"—a review of change drivers and their impact, both positive and negative, on your business—into every agenda, from the board meeting to the Monday departmental get-together. Encourage everyone to contribute his own foresight. Make it part of the regular conversation.

By making the wake-up call part of your regular work, you are in effect reconditioning yourself and your company culture so that it perpetually faces forward, rather than inward or backward. This exercise keeps your mind limber. It keeps your team stimulated and motivated to be agile. Because when it's time to innovate and harness the mass movement for good, everyone knows the answer to the biggest question of all, which is always "why?"

Your customers are waking up. Your employees are waking up. Your suppliers are too, and the communities in which you operate. The conflux has opened our eyes, and in our broad and bright awakening, a new culture, a Culture of Conscience, is emerging.

3

The Culture of Conscience

IT'S enough to kick off a revolution: zero privacy threatening our personal liberty, rising sea levels threatening our homes, and a rising tide of rage at accelerating income disparity, among other things. Our interconnectedness has heightened our awareness of the impact we—and the businesses from which we buy, for which we work, and in which we invest—have on humanity and our planet. This in turn intensifies the demand for positive agency and meaning not only in what we do but in all the decisions we make. It's a clear meta-trend, a mass movement for good, that's been gaining momentum for forty years.

And now, the movement is reaching its tipping point. Broad awareness of social injustices and environmental risks, concurrent with emerging technology innovations, has given rise to new rules, expectations, behaviors, participants, and structures. And the conflux of forces that are redefining how we live, interact, work, and play are giving rise to a new global culture. This emergent culture—the Culture of Conscience—is all around us; indeed, we already inhabit it.

A Culture of Conscience is taking hold so broadly that some might dismiss it as too ubiquitous to characterize as a sociologically momentous event. But with it comes new priorities and accountabilities that are steadily transforming the way we work, live, prosper, and measure success. The consequences are not confined to one or two business sectors; indeed, every business, large and small, will be affected by it. It's an epochal cultural shift. The question is, how will *your* business thrive in it?

The values and assumptions that are fueling a new wave of business innovation are highly distinct from the system that preceded them. The next generation of leaders and managers, those young people who have grown up with high-speed connectivity as a basic utility, and with access to and the ability to manipulate media as a basic assumption, already believe it's possible to catalyze broad and positive change, both as individuals and through their engagement with business. They readily assume the responsibility of their own power to change the world with the casual effortlessness of riding a bicycle.

But moving from one culture to another can be disorienting, to say the least. The most perplexing—and for business, failure-inducing—aspects of a new or different culture can be the very things you don't see. A new culture doesn't always induce culture shock. Far worse is culture *blindness*.

I moved from California to London a decade ago, and I thought I was merely moving my belongings to a place where people had charming accents, sipped tea, and were unfailingly polite. Like all American arrivals, I assumed that beyond these quaint and aspirational cultural tics, my new neighbors and colleagues and community were mostly just like me—English-speaking people who listened to the same music and watched the same movies and television. As far as I could tell, I had no reason to consider changing the way I worked. I had always gotten great feedback on the way I communicate, collaborate, and lead.

And so, with this assumption in mind, I acted exactly as I would in San Francisco. I remember one of my first business meetings in the London office. I started it with typical American can-do. With a broad grin, fists confidently resting on the conference table, I boomed out "Okay, team, together we're gonna make this thing HAPPEN!"

If you're British, or if you've lived and worked in Britain, you are already grimacing. If you haven't, here's a tip: the last thing you should do in the culture of the United Kingdom is to start a business meeting with boisterous cheerleading. In fact, it's unwise to start a business meeting with any business at all. Here, in this gentler, more subtle and tactful culture, you need warm up first. So, you start by talking perhaps about the incessant rain, a few minor frustrations, and even perhaps your hangover. You offer a biscuit (a cookie) and pour some tea. But never, ever, "Go team!"

At the time, my leadership style in the United States was seen at best as cheerleader-coach-optimist and at worst as highly focused and perfectionist. But in the U.K., I was perceived to be fake, unrealistic, and overbearing. I had no idea. Until the company, wisely, sent me off to cultural training. Really, it was cultural reconditioning. It changed everything.

Here's the thing. One of the trickiest situations for individuals and businesses is the sudden immersion in a culture that *looks* familiar but is utterly different. It's why cross-cultural understanding has been an imperative for global corporations for decades. Geert Hofstede shed light on cultural dissonance in his cultural dimensions theory, a framework for cross-cultural understanding and communication that emerged from his work with IBM in the 1960s and 1970s. His research and analysis established a means of understanding differences in values and assumptions across a range of dimensions, from power to uncertainty to indulgence, many of which are invisible, operating below the surface of directly perceived behavior.

And thus, the most powerful lesson I learned in my course, from a charismatic coach named Matthew Hill, is something called the Iceberg Model.

Consider an iceberg. Actually, consider two icebergs, floating lazily in the sea. There's what you see above the surface, shining white in the Arctic sunshine, and there's what you don't see below the water's surface, which is where most of the mass lies.

"Cultures are like icebergs," Matthew told me. "There's what you see, and there's what you don't see, but it's all part of the whole. And like an iceberg, most of it, you can't detect." The undetectable? That's the deep stuff. Years of unspoken assumptions. Personal and collective experiences that shape those assumptions. Value systems held so close to the heart that, although they inform everything, they might be and usually are utterly invisible to the visitor.

The U.K. and the U.S. are a unique pair of icebergs, unique in the world, in fact. Because what you see—the shape of the icebergs above the surface of the water—is so very similar. Similar foods, popular media, and interests. Lots of mutual admiration and co-opting of symbols. But what's under the surface is as different as any alien culture's. Even the same words have different meanings. "Are you alright?" in the U.S. means that the asker is concerned that you might be ill. In the U.K., the question means "How are you doing today?" The underlying differences between the U.K. and the U.S. are indeed as vast as the differences between, say, the U.S. and Russia or the U.S. and Nigeria.

When cultures *seem* so similar but are in fact so very different at the core, migration from one to the other is even more challenging than when the expectation is that the culture to which you're migrating is dramatically and visibly different. In other words, because I'd expect it to be tough to live in Lagos, Nigeria, my adjustment wouldn't be as difficult. I'd automatically know that I needed to change my behavior, modulate my voice, and learn the rules before speaking out. Because if I didn't, I'd likely fail. Or at least, alienate nearly everyone.

Here's why this is important to understand.

When you look around yourself, even though you're living in it, the Conscience Culture doesn't *look* very different from the business environment to which we're accustomed. The most significant changes—dramatic, deeply felt, and probably permanent—are not visible on the surface. Life looks more or less as it did before. People seem to be behaving in similar ways. They work, they shop, they drive, they stress out, they go to the movies.

It doesn't look like anything dramatic is going on. Or does it? Gay weddings conducted on a live broadcast of the Grammys in 2014? Even I wouldn't have predicted that. But there are other signs of change too. Supermarket shelf space expands dramatically for organic produce in mainstream supermarkets—including at Walmart and Kroger. McDonald's offers Rainforest Alliance-certified espresso. An African American descendant of slaves serves as First Lady in the White House. Social media and content-sharing rises exponentially, absorbing increasing hours of our leisure (and work) time. A closer inspection of everyday life yields richer evidence of what's happening below the surface. So let's take a tour of the most indicative aspects of this new culture. I've clustered them under three categories: beliefs, expectations, and players. And I invite you, as you peruse them, to consider where you and your business stand, on a virtual sliding scale, in relation to each.

Conscience Culture Beliefs

These are the emergent core beliefs and motivations that propel behavior and inform life choices—how to connect and communicate, what to buy, how to make a living.

Collective Self-Actualization

"What's good for we is good for me." The emergent culture is deeply self-centered. But that "self" at the center is a different construct from that which preceded it. It's a collective self. Me as *we*.

Psychologist Abraham Maslow missed a layer in his iconic pyramid of the hierarchy of human needs, which, in a typically Western-inflected logic, put personal self-actualization at the pinnacle. As the theory goes, we're unlikely to pursue higher levels of needs in the pyramid until we've fulfilled those at the foundation, like food, shelter, and belonging. There are two things Maslow couldn't have considered: the implications of global interconnectivity and interdependence, and the increasing prevalence of a non-Western and more collective self-orientation.

For a new generation raised with social connectivity and hooked on social media, the boundaries between "me" and "we" are blurrier than ever before. Tightly interwoven and continuously reaffirmed affiliation with family, friends, and a tribe of like-minded people has generated a collective sense of "self." And thus, we don't self-actualize alone, we expect to do it together. Even personalized solutions—playlists, outfits, bicycles, cars—are built on a backbone of social recommendations and group approval. The new baseline assumption is: what's good for you is also good for me. And its corollary is: I want what's good for me to be good for you too. It doesn't mean that there's no place for competitiveness or individuality. Far from it. It means that improving life for others is as important as improving ourselves. Businesses that not only appeal to this motivation in their communications but offer solutions that allow it to be enacted are poised to thrive. Businesses that engender a deeply felt sense of shared mission will be poised to attract and keep the most talented and committed employees.

Optimism

"We can create a better world. So we will." Young populations in high-growth markets are positively exuberant, believing (often for good reason) that the quality of their lives will be better than that of their parents, and that the future will be brighter than the past. Remember Amit and Raghuvesh, whom we visited in Delhi in chapter 1? Yes even in recession-prone Europe and America, millennials believe that it *should* be possible to improve their world.

Optimism can, and does, breed frustration when the rest of society doesn't join the party. Because a core assumption in the Conscience Culture is that everyone can and should focus on making life better for all. And businesses have a special responsibility to do so. That means yours. Optimistic businesses have a clear, jargon-free vision of their role in a better world, and they discuss it publicly all the time. Which means that their fans discuss that vision, and that business, too. You don't have to be a technology company—indeed, it's even more interesting if you're not—to be in the middle of the cultural conversation about changing the world.

Fairness

"Everyone has the right to live a great life. Everyone." Nothing outrages the new culture more than sheer unfairness. Everyone has a right to a decent life. This is obvious, as one example, in the international outrage that boiled over on social media over Russia's policies around gay "propaganda" as the country hosted the 2014 Winter Olympics. It's also what's driving the "equality" movement (which I'd prefer we re-dub the "fairness movement"). The new culture is by no means anti-success (that corner of the debate is coming from an older and frankly more bitter generation). Mark Zuckerberg, who with his wife has just topped the 2013 *Chronicle of Philanthropy* list of top donors, is a hero (and a villain). The transparent justification for the pricing of your products and services, the consequences of your manufacturing and supply chain, and your company's role in empowering and liberating increasing numbers of people are all domains for harnessing the emotional pull of fairness.

Well-Being

"We expect to be and feel healthy in body, mind, and spirit." In the Culture of Conscience, all products and services should enable better health and well-being. This is a culture that wants to know how its food was produced. A culture that creates and pursues health fads with a vengeance, from superfoods to fasting to gluten-free products. No couch potatoes here; triathlons, mountain treks, music festivals, and overseas adventures are the province of leisure time. Bicycling is a veritable symbol of the culture. From workouts to yoga to meditation to spiritual and religious community participation, well-being is at the core of the agenda. Health care is a right, not a privilege. What are you doing for your employees? What's your position on the issue, and why? Because it's going to get talked about by your next wave of customers.

Transparency

"We crave knowing everything, so if you don't tell us, we'll find out for ourselves." Here's a direct consequence of the Internet—the expectation that all should be knowable, discoverable, seeable. Even if you, as a business, don't provide information about yourself, it's going to get hacked, found out, discovered, broadcast. Calories, sodium, and fat. Environmental and social impact. Employee policies. Factory conditions.

But transparency is about more than sharing information. It's about breaking down the walls of your business. Think open-kitchen restaurant. So open up: encourage us to explore your business like we're a part of it, because we are. Show off your shining production line. Let us get to know your people. Bring us into the boardroom and the R&D lab. If you've already patented it, why not let us get our hands on it? We'll help you turn it into something we need. Make transparency an everyday operating procedure.

Authenticity

"We see right through fake, so keep it real." A subset of transparency, this is both behavioral and material. It was recent big news when a haul of "cashmere" scarves turned out to have been woven from rat fur. Unsavory product adulterations are nothing new, but they've also never been easier to discover and broadcast than they are now. An authentic company is a trustworthy company. And in this culture, trust is the paramount currency.

Authenticity is conveyed through material ingredients and processes, too. In categories like food, artisanal small-batch is a paragon of authenticity. But high-tech materials and mass production are equally authentic when there's a really good reason to innovate with them. See the previous section on transparency. Even a single authentic ingredient or component can make all the difference in the perception of your value. Your quality of construction adds to your value—not only in terms of product robustness, but as a sustainability message—because planned obsolescence is arguably unethical from a resource perspective. Clarifying consumer understanding about where you produce, and why, can add to your value. Even factory robots can be authentic, when we get to know them. And even "artificially flavored" can be authentic, if you celebrate it. See "irreverence," below.

Disruptive Irreverence

"Let's turn it all upside down." No system, business model, or tradition is immune to irreverent reinvention in the new culture. Everything is up for disruption; indeed, substantial energy goes toward finding new sectors to reinvent. Hotels? Let's rent a guest room on Airbnb instead. Taxi transport? Why not carpool instead?

Meanwhile, holier-than-thou political correctness is a turnoff. The lighthearted buzz of irreverence is far more fun and insouciant. It's a sign of self-empowerment, because the empowered citizen can afford to laugh. Indeed, the Culture of Conscience is light, because people feel they can make a difference. It loves to be a little naughty. It loves to show off its newest tattoo and its latest scrape-up from the skateboard. It reads *Vice*. So don't preach to the world how lofty your company's environmental track record is. Grin and admit to us how badass you are as you protect the planet. And make sure you understand how your own sector is going to get kicked around—and either get ahead of it, engage in it, or batten down the hatches, because it's inevitable.

Sensible Environmentalism

"If it's bad for the planet, it's not for us." 'Nuff said. Note the word sensible. "Responsible" is patronizing and out of sync with the new culture. The next generation wasn't introduced to environmentalism as a fringe movement; they grew up with it as a given. The more your business does to operate in an environmentally sensible way, the more contemporary (read: sexy) it is. It's not a cost center or a sideline activity. Alternative energy is today an aspiration more than an everyday reality for most of us, but the demand will rise in the wake of continued climate change. According to the U.S. Energy Information Administration, the market for renewable energy is forecast to grow steadily year over year. Renewable energy sources already drive upward of 12 percent of U.S. electricity supply. Nothing says "modern success" like a roof paved with solar panels. And nothing says "we care" more than an ecologically sensible headquarters.

Throughout its decade-long reign as the world's mobile phone leader, Nokia was also the leader in sustainability. Make environmental sensibility a core principle of your innovation agenda, invest in it, and you might discover, as Procter & Gamble recently did, better, lower-cost materials. Mayakoba, a resort in Cancun, has differentiated itself and attracted some of the world's most high-net-worth travelers, who are drawn to the biodiversity of wetlands the resort protected, areas that would have otherwise been overdeveloped. Environmentalism can be the business value driver.

Global Citizenship

"We are part of something bigger." The old trope "think globally, act locally" is being turned on its head. Now, it's "think locally, act globally." We focus on our immediate community because that's where we live. But we buy things that signify our participation in broader movements and aspirations. Even local neighborhoods (right now, it's Brooklyn) become globally aspirational, inspiring restaurants, retail concepts, fashion, and lifestyle. In fast-developing markets, the adoption of global products, services, and values is a sign of sophistication and upward mobility.

To stay in sync with the culture, your business should adopt a way of working that synthesizes localized thinking with global action. Local knowledge and empathy for local value systems is vital. But high-value brands will refuse to adapt to local values when those values are wildly out of sync with broader and more aspirational global belief systems. Sexism, for example, is just not a good global look. Meanwhile, make your own local knowledge, sourcing, manufacturing, operations, and people a part of your appeal. Even brag about it! "Proudly made by Anya, mother of two kids we're helping send to school."

Conscience Culture Expectations

Conscience Culture thrives in the near-complete synthesis of virtual technology and the physical world. Its denizens are the most tech-savvy of populations, and their lives are saturated with innovative technology, yet they also place a higher-than-average value on remaining present in the real and natural world. This is a culture that systemically rediscovers and restores physical spaces, time-honored traditions, foods, and manufacturing processes. You might call the people at the forefront of this culture *hipsters,* and you wouldn't be wrong. They believe that small-scale organic farming is glamorous, cheese making is noble, and vinyl delivers better audio quality.

So it's not impossible to envision a resurgence of paper and print. The moans about the end of print have filled the mediasphere since the launch of *Wired* magazine. ("Why paper?" the founders were consistently asked twenty years ago. "Because it's still the best technology for delivering high-resolution, portable, and interactive information that's not dependent on a battery" was the answer.) Admittedly, many currently reject paper in favor of e-reading, but given the tendency, in our virtualizing world, to celebrate the merits of physicality and craftsmanship, it might be only a matter of time before this new culture adopts and subsequently renews paper—perhaps embedded with digital capabilities—as the ultimate interactive material. After all, re-shoring and near-shoring of both paper recycling and printing processes will streamline print production and distribution.

The following technology enablers make this synthesis of physical and digital experience possible.

Mobile Connectedness

"I never stand still. I take it all with me, everywhere." Smartphones introduced us to a whole new way of connecting and computing. Cloud computing makes data and media even more portable. Multiscreen, multi-speaker—it's not just about seeing, but hearing, too. We want to port our content, productivity, and identity across multiple devices and contexts. And we want to do it in multiple ways. Sometimes we'll carry it, sometimes we'll wear it, sometimes we'll leave all the gear at home except for a "key" and access our own stuff elsewhere.

The next chapter of mobility? Mobilizing place-based domains like learning, healing, banking, governing. The new hardware? Cars, public transport, airplane seats. Why is mobility an enabler of Conscience Culture? Because it liberates people to get out into the real world and even up in the air without leaving the empowerment of connected information behind. It provides affordable access to information and resources on low-cost devices. It improves driver safety by detecting road (and driver) conditions and enabling the vehicle and the driver to adapt. Shortly after off-loading its handset manufacturing division to Microsoft, Nokia announced a $100 million fund for start-ups focused on optimizing the in-car computing and location-based experience, suggesting a new locus for mobile innovation beyond the smartphone. The bigger question here: Is policy (transportation law, safety standards, privacy protection, and so on) keeping pace?

Do you have a robust mobile strategy, one that goes beyond a mere shopping app or mobile-friendly website? Because the portability of information offers more than an in-everyone's-pocket advertising channel—indeed, marketing that interrupts or creates a lag between intention and action is set to fail. But mobile capability can nudge you and your customers closer together in the real world. Virtual reality on a tablet or smartphone can enable your customers to see through walls (and packaging) and gain a better understanding of you and your offering. Location-based services on a map interface can guide customers to services they need—power charging, ATMs, bathrooms—thus creating an association between your brand and the help that the customer needs.

Human Connection

"I don't buy what businesses say. I buy what real people say." We turn to one another—to wikis, to our Twitter stream, to Instagram. We want personal points of view, recommendations, social graphs, customer service, the Apple Genius bar. Why is human connection a Conscience Culture enabler? Because conscience itself is human, and cannot be calculated and conveyed through an algorithm. At least not yet. Human intuition, emotion, and experience are effective outcome predictors, as Malcolm Gladwell spelled out in his landmark book *Blink: The Power of Thinking Without Thinking*. Our brains are adept at processing multiple multisensory inputs like facial expressions and body language, and interpolating them with personal history and experience. Face-to-face is still the most effective means of communication. And there's nothing more conscientious than bringing people into closer contact with one another. How human is your business? How authentic and empathetic are your service people? Is your business enabling customers to meet one another and you? Where are the points of human contact? Are you cutting them? Or increasing them?

Contextual Relevance

"Give me everything I need but only precisely when and where I need it." It's not that we've become greedy or picky. It's that our mobile devices are equipped with a range of GPS and other contextual sensors and supported by intelligent Internet services that can self-adjust to our location, our behavior habits, and our circumstance. It means that we have every reason to expect that businesses will only provide us what we need, when we need it. No more clutter, interruption, or distraction. Real-time data can be automatically filtered and adapted to address where you are, what you're doing, who you're with, what your intent is, and what someone else's intent is for you. How can your business eliminate its information clutter, and instead deliver only the relevant message at the right moment, the moment when it's most needed and most likely to be acted upon?

Actionability

"We don't just want to know it. We want to do something about it." A friend tells me a story of how his two-year-old was in tears the first time she experienced a flat-panel TV, because when she touched the screen, nothing happened. The age of the passive "consumer" is over. The new culture is used to making things happen at the touch of a finger. They create, remix, remake, and broadcast their own media. They use apps to impact what happens to them next, wherever they are. They bake from scratch. They start companies. They overthrow governments with their mobile phones. They transform anything they can get their hands on. How can your business make it easier for people to make an impact on their lives—how can you help them start a business, change their community, or create something new, whether it's a meal, a piece of music, or a program that helps their community? Are your solutions—and your communication—immediately actionable?

Smarter Everything

"We expect everything—our house, car, bike, gear—to learn from us and get smarter." For years, the Internet of Things was a conceptual prediction, but Google's recent $3.2 billion acquisition of Nest, the smart thermostat, has put it squarely in the center of the next wave of business innovation. What types of products and services could be augmented by smarter hardware? And what objects could gain new value by becoming smart themselves?

It's time for all businesses to plan for the Internet of Things. Because businesses that make physical products should consider how those objects can become smarter, more useful, and more valuable. Cars and home appliances like washing machines and refrigerators will be among the first in this wave, but it's set to impact everything—as in, the stuff that's *in* the car, refrigerator, and washing machine. When a customer is considering your product, its smartness will be as much a factor in the decision as its quality and price. And businesses that provide services must consider how those services can be enhanced and even delivered by smart objects. Smartness will be the new core utility.

Adjustable Anonymity

"We expect to decide who knows us and what they do with that knowledge." Young people are turning away from the massive Class of 198X High School Reunion that is Facebook (after all, it's populated with millions of middle-aged gen Xers like me), and interacting with each other on more ephemeral platforms like Instagram and Snapchat. The next frontier of innovation in networked connectivity will be the development of solutions that offer greater anonymity, fluidity, and individual control of our identity management. Peer-to-peer solutions, self-destructing communications, and biometric log-ins will be key ingredients in the new anonymity. There is significant business opportunity in solving a current quandary: how to deliver the accessibility benefits of the cloud (a new generation is happy to expose much of themselves in return for a positive benefit) while negating the hazards of exposure and its potential to overstep personal civil liberty.

Customization and Personalization

"We'll hack it, build on it, take it apart, remake it, personalize it." The open source movement started it, and its consequences continue. The new assumption is that anything can be toyed with, adjusted, remade, reused, upcycled, fixed, recoded. Increasingly affordable and accessible 3D printing will bring open source thinking to the physical world. And our understanding of the genetic code, which will soon be supplemented with more health data collected by connected biosensors, means that biological innovation is set to be open sourceable too. How intentionally open and hackable are your products or services? How radically open could they be?

Shareable Content

"If it's not shareable, it's not worth it." First it was media—pictures, music tracks, recipes. Now it's physical stuff too. Our cars, our homes, our commutes. Coworking spaces. Why own when you can share? This trend suggests the beginning of a shift in the very notion of ownership. We're moving steadily toward content and service subscription models and other systems that facilitate sharing. From music that we "rent" and stream to homes that we can trade with others, the sharing phenomenon—and new business models that support it—is on the rise. Digital information and online identity management ensure that we have portability, fluidity, and transparency, three key ingredients in making it possible to share goods, services, spaces, and media. This will give rise to all sorts of new service providers that make sharing easier, less risky, and more fun.

Competitive Fun

"Entertain us, or else we'll entertain ourselves." Previous generations universally, if begrudgingly, accepted that some aspects of life—work, for example—just weren't going to be fun. Suffering was tolerated as a fact of life. But a new generation has never been weaned off the immediate and free gratification of always-available entertainment. Gamification will spread into the sphere of social and environmental benefit. Why is this part of Conscience Culture? Because when something is addictively fun and even more importantly, visibly and socially competitive, people are motivated to participate in it and advocate for their performance in it with more zeal. Competitive fun breaks down barriers between people or communities and those things they don't really want to do. Getting to know your own health, improving leadership skills, supporting social entrepreneurs, monitoring microinvestments—all of these things could be gamified. Could filing taxes become a source of competitive pride? How can you build more playfulness, humor, and motivation into your products, services, and communications? Because when you do so, you nudge people toward behaviors that are not only better for them but better for your profit margin. And when something is fun, and when we get ourselves onto the leaderboard doing it, we are more likely to talk about it.

Beauty Matters

"Good design shows that you care about us." Aesthetics aren't skin deep; they are part of our quality of life. Design savvy and visually fluent, the new culture talks in pictures, on Snapchat and Instagram. Do your brand and your products convey stylish swagger, aspirational pull? Your product had better have a style that says and means something. This means that your business has to stay in tune with the shifts of fashion and the cutting edge of visual culture, and intentionally position itself either knowingly apart from or directly within it. This is not only critical for product companies, by the way—it's also crucial for service businesses. Distinctive design shows that you solve problems elegantly. Style shows you have a point of view. It attracts talented employees as well as dedicated customers. And it looks good on Instagram—a picture is worth a thousand tweets. In the Conscience Economy, these considerations are not superficial. A better world is a more beautiful world.

Conscience Culture Players

There is such a wide-ranging and continuously expanding cast of players that it would be impossible to commit a complete list to print. But what they all have in common is a mission for good. Here are some categories of key players today.

Social Enterprises and Incubators

A hybrid of for-profit commerce and social-impact agenda, it's been estimated that social enterprises already contribute upward of $200 billion to the U.S. economy. They can take some of the strain off of overstretched public programs (which is why the U.K. government invests in them).

One of the first and most famous social enterprises was the restaurant Fifteen, founded by celebrity chef Jamie Oliver. It's not only a successful restaurant (years later, it's still tough to get a reservation), it's famous for its apprentice program, which trains young people who, in Oliver's words, "have faced enormous challenges in their lives," helping them enter society with both professional skills and dignity. The restaurant donates all of its profits to charity while enhancing the Jamie Oliver brand emblazoned across his for-profit businesses. But the model does generate profit and has inspired a new generation of people to imagine and build enterprises that have positive social impact at their core. Ben & Jerry's (prior to its acquisition by Unilever) was also considered a pioneer in social enterprise, with its emphasis on the "double bottom line" and the socially progressive mission that was not only stated as its core but delivered through its supply chain.

Social enterprise harnesses the passion and energy of entrepreneurship as a force for good. At an event where the newest round of social enterprises (those that had won a spot in Telefónica's prestigious program) were making their pitches, the energy was amazing. "Every dollar, pound, or euro you spend is a vote," one of the young founders explained to the packed room, "but most of us don't know what value system or social or environmental consequence we're voting for. Our software will reveal it, so you can use your votes the way you want to." He was offering a contextual, mobile decision engine based on personal values. Only a Culture of Conscience could generate such an innovation. Are you engaging with social enterprise? Are you learning from it? Could part of your business even become one?

Certification Associations

"Badness-free accountability." "Green" products—from chocolate to detergent—promote the notion that by buying them, we are minimizing harm to people and the environment. Fair Trade certification—in which companies are audited by Fair Trade USA and earn the right to use the Fair Trade Certified label—has been one of the more successful of these models. It's widely recognized and well branded, and the term has become part of the general lexicon for many people. But even the Fair Trade model, though in my opinion a laudable advance, is an economically imperfect system, as it arguably manipulates pricing albeit for a humane purpose. Carbon offsetting, the ability to "offset" your "carbon footprint" by funding programs that, through a carefully thought-out calculation, claim to put things right again, sends a good message, but does offsetting really solve the root cause of the problem it highlights?

Today, there are a range of recognizable labels and certification standards, including organic, cruelty free, and Fair Trade. These indicators vary country by country (as indeed the regulatory and legal environments in which they exist vary, too) and it's worth noting that some are actual enforceable standards imposed by government, some have been created by voluntary certification bodies, and others are marketing signals with no legally enforceable accountability. Still, they proliferate.

Consumers are drawn to them, and indeed, they help brands signify good intent. But great as they are as signposts of conscientiousness, the efficacy and accuracy of these marks will continue to come under increasing scrutiny.

Given the dynamics of social media and the increasing availability of real-time information, it's possible that in the near future more decentralized "associations" will assess and approve supply chain processes and corporate operations. Just as traffic maps can be crowdsourced, roving virtual bands of citizens aligned with a common purpose and incentivized to be vigilant could improve accountability and efficacy of production and trade processes.

Goodness Marketplaces

"Where to buy and sell good goods." These marketplaces, both online and real world, aggregate conscientiously sourced and created products and experiences. Etsy started the online trend and continues to be among the most visible brands, although a 2013 update of its guidelines, downplaying "handmade" products and focusing instead on "unique" products has resulted in an exodus of many of its original vendors. These revised definitions and subsequent terms of service have enabled mass producers of cheap imports, many from Asia, to promote their goods on the site (which are, as you'd imagine, priced considerably lower than the artisanal products upon which Etsy built its initial brand). The controversy is instructive, as it has created opportunities for emerging online marketplaces and communities like Zibbet, DoGoodBuyUs, and Fashioning Change.

Outgrow.me merges the concept of a goodness marketplace with crowdfunding, featuring Kickstarter-funded products. (Warning: it includes so much well-designed and well-intentioned innovation that it's addictive.)

Goodness marketplaces also include physical retailers committed to selling conscientious goods and services, from farmers markets and small-scale retailers to Whole Foods (I can't resist noting the irony of their seeming monopoly on the goodness category) to the School of Life. The latter is both an actual storefront in London and an online community that sells learning experiences. These experiences include field trips with experts and Sunday morning "sermons," which are decidedly secular TED Talk–style lectures from thinkers, artists, and philosophers.

How might your products qualify to be included in such marketplaces, or could you build or enable one yourself?

Democratizing Enablers

"Accessible impact." Domains of human endeavor that were once inaccessible or reserved only for the elite are becoming available to all. Crowdfunding and microfinancing are modalities for providing direct fiscal support to entrepreneurs as well as causes that we personally believe in. They're evidence of this desire to enact something, to impact directly rather than relying on secondary or tertiary impact. Out of this desire comes the "frugal tech" movement, with its mission to provide the benefits of computing with extremely low-cost materials. Among the movement's successes is Raspberry Pi—developed by the nonprofit Raspberry Pi Foundation—a low-cost single-board computer that empowers children to learn computer programming. Meanwhile, online communities like iFixit.org are harbingers of an increasing desire to collectively and individually repair and extend the usefulness of the things we already own.

Built-In Philanthropy

"Helping by buying." This arena includes what are currently called "one-for-one businesses," like TOMS Shoes and One Water. You buy a bottle of water and you concurrently give a bottle of water. In the case of One Water, some of the purchase price funds the renovation of a village water pump in sub-Saharan Africa. It's an easy model for consumers to understand, although TOMS Shoes—which provides a pair of shoes for the poor for every pair you buy, found itself criticized for not addressing the root cause of poverty. The company promptly adjusted its model with TOMS Glasses, which supports and funds vision care in disadvantaged communities rather than providing a straight product-for-product donation.

These models aren't easy to sustain, particularly in the FMCG (fast-moving consumer goods) category. One Water has struggled to get footing in supermarkets because mass retailers that carry FMCG products force margin down so low that it's next to impossible to make a profit while delivering the social benefit. But people will pay for brand prestige, and context is everything. Starbucks carries One Water because of the premium and conscientious message it sends about the Starbucks brand.

Other emergent in-built philanthropy models are experimenting with incentives that facilitate automated micro-donations to social or environmental causes. For example, Mogl, a restaurant loyalty app in California, automatically donates a percentage of your restaurant bill to feeding people. You collect "meals donated" instead of points, so that the amount that you give is a new kind of "loyalty" currency. It's an effortless incentive to use the service and eat out more—and it's a differentiator for the service provider and the participating restaurants, as well as a braggable for the person using it.

Impact Investing and Socially Responsible Investing Vehicles

"Investing for the common good as well as a good return." Impact investing is both a philosophical approach to investing and a fast-growing category of financial instruments. Unlike socially responsible investing (SRI), which uses a negative screen to avoid certain investments, this type of investing deploys a proactive approach, a positive screening process, to solve social and environmental problems. Both types are growing, and if you surf the financial and investment press, you'll quickly see that both are buzzy, even if some of the parameters to describe them are fuzzy.

Here's what catches my eye, though: although they don't always deliver a competitive return, these vehicles continue to attract investment, suggesting that some investors value more than personal gain. Research by JP Morgan and the Global Impact Investment Network showed that investor groups had planned to commit $9 billion to this asset class in 2013. In India alone, the impacting investing category has been estimated to be growing by 30 percent annually. According to an article in the *Financial Times,* it's difficult to measure the size of the category, but one estimate suggests that impact investing could attract upward of $1 trillion over the next ten years. Socially responsible investing leads the trend; by 2012, more than $3.7 trillion was invested in this category in the U.S. alone, and the growth continues.

In traditional investing, decision factors boiled down to a simple binary truth: "either you make money or you don't." In the Conscience Economy, it's "you make money and make a difference, or you make more money and pass on the real costs to others." This is an evolution worth watching because it signals a motivational shift among a particularly rigorous and demanding sector of people. Huge gains are not the only investment motivator, which suggests that in the future there might be different kinds of profit. Emotional profit and time profit, for example. It's been called the next revolution in finance, following on the heels of venture capital as a major driver of innovation and economic transformation.

Media

"The voices of the movement." Trade publications like *CSRWire* and *Business Ethics*, aimed at CSR professionals and sustainability specialists, have proliferated for more than a decade. More recently, new consumer lifestyle media properties like GOOD.is, SHFT, and Upworthy appeal to a young cohort driven by a passion for making a positive difference in the world. TED Talks have become a widely respected forum for Conscience Culture ideas to get airplay. But mainstream media brands regularly report on increasingly conscientious business and social phenomena, too. Not a day goes by when I don't spot something in the news, in the media, or online that expresses a Conscience Culture point of view, whether it's a story about renewable energy, genetic engineering, food safety and security, social entrepreneurship, ethical (or unethical) business practices, conscientious consumerism, diversity in the boardroom, dilemmas of sensor technology and privacy, or debates on financial reform.

Role Models

"Thinking big, speaking out, giving back." Visionary business leaders and entertainment celebrities personify the status aspirations and lifestyles of the new culture. Although philanthropy as an overt demonstration of wealth goes back generations, there is a renewed glamour associated with making a real difference in the world. Many of our most admired role models now augment their glamour and success by using it to advocate for and support social good. Whether establishing major foundations, building schools, adopting a virtual Benetton advertisement of diverse children into their families, becoming U.N. Goodwill Ambassadors, or speaking out on topical human rights and environmental issues, the world's most visible and famous people are no longer mere paragons of success, wealth, and sex appeal.

Actors Jane Fonda and Paul Newman may have been the forebears of this new kind of fame. Steve Jobs brought rock star status to visionary tech leadership. Today, new entrepreneurs like Lauren Bush Lauren and Blake Mycoskie are heroes among a generation of socially motivated entrepreneurs as they each build ventures that seek to convert consumers into cause-oriented donors and community participants. At the 2014 SXSW (South By Southwest) conference, septuagenarian *Star Trek* veteran and social media sensation George Takei did a standing-room-only interview, dazzling thousands of fans with his no-nonsense message of diversity. (Shout-outs from the audience included "Run for office, George!") Edward Snowden, divisive among some, is an iconic voice for those concerned about what's happening with our online data. Even Pope Francis has impressed a new generation of nonreligious people with his media savvy and his leaning toward inclusivity. Perhaps more than ever before, status and celebrity are enmeshed with a call to change the world for the better.

Professional Services and Consultancies

"Helping make it happen." A broad range of specialized professional services have been evolving for over a decade. Most were purpose-built to bring professional strategy support, management advice, business reengineering expertise, financial analysis, and marketing communication support to nonprofit organizations. The expertise is beginning to move in the other direction; knowledge gained in the public and nonprofit sectors is increasingly applicable to for-profit businesses.

This category of service providers includes CSR strategy agencies, design firms, sustainability consultancies, social impact practices within the big management consultancies, and environmental and cause marketing agencies.

Staying Relevant

Obviously, any business needs to be relevant in the wider culture in which it exists. This means operating in sync within the cultural value system, meeting and exceeding cultural expectations, and being one of its players. The most robust businesses are those that not only function within the culture but drive it forward. By leading the next wave, your business can become an icon of it. Iconic businesses dominate public and customer conversation; they are included by default at the forefront of people's minds when it's time to make a purchase decision. They are thus more likely to be chosen, and enjoy significant leads in value share in their categories.

Some businesses are closer to future-proof category leadership in the Conscience Economy than others (Whole Foods in the supermarket category, Google in technology, TOMS Shoes in one-to-one), but no company has secured its position yet. Even those out in front have their vulnerabilities—for example, for Whole Foods, it's pricing (is there anyone who *doesn't* call it "Whole Paycheck?") and some of its business practices, and for Google, increasing privacy and monopoly concerns. In the race for dominance in the emergent culture, the top spots across the Conscience Economy are still up for grabs. The only way to get there is to directly incorporate the emergent beliefs and expectations into your own business, and to simultaneously determine what kind of player (or players) your business can be.

A new generation believes in the imminent possibility of a better world, and they're determined to manifest it. The culture they inhabit— a culture that's quickly becoming mainstream—will be the context in which your business needs to thrive. And in order to do so, you will need to attract people not only with the utility of your product or solution but, even more crucially, with the emotional magnetism of your brand.

4

The Cult of Brand Belief

Every culture features its own brands—if you can even recognize them. I've rented a flat in Spain on Airbnb, and I need to buy a bottle of bleach. Problemo: no hablo español. I squint and scan the shelves looking for brands I recognize—Domestos? Clorox? Nope. I look for packaging that seems similar to bleach I've bought in the past—bottle shapes, colors. Useless. Finally, I pull out my iPhone, look up the Spanish word for bleach, and start reading labels. The whole process takes four times longer than merely grabbing what's familiar. Guilt sets in. I probably shouldn't even be using bleach, but a more environmentally sensible alternative. I end up buying the cheapest bottle and walk out feeling uneasy. Imagine every purchase decision taking this much time, and with so little conviction on the buyer's part.

A world without familiar brands is an alien place. Imagine a supermarket with no labels on any of the products. Now put the labels back on, but no brands. How much reading would you need to do to find what you need? This is the simple reason that brands are here to stay. And they're about to become more important than ever.

Our brains are designed to filter and forget. It's been said that if we remembered every detail of everything we encounter, we'd go insane. We simply aren't capable of remembering all the details of our life experiences, just as we don't remember every dream we have. But we do remember people, faces, identities. We develop rich associations and allegiances based upon the totality of experiences shared. I may not remember a single aspect of every experience I've shared with my best friend, but I see her and I feel great affection. It is much the same with brands. They are summations, an easy-to-recognize shorthand.

Brands have become much more than a shorthand for price and efficacy, although those are indeed part of the picture. Today, brands trigger *feelings*, which are our gut response to the sum of everything we have learned, experienced, heard, and know about a particular company. Brands are the best means of securing emotional attachment to business (or place, or political movement, or whatever the sector is). And given that it's been estimated that 80 percent of decision making is ultimately emotional, while 20 percent is rational, managing the emotional magnetism of your brand is your most important, value-creating business process.

This is because citizens of Conscience Culture wear their values on their sleeves—and carry them in their pockets, slip them into their tablet cases, fill their baskets with them at the market, download them to their smartphones, and post about them on social media. The values they uphold are signified and expressed through the brands they choose, use, promote, and join as employees.

Show me the brands you most love and use, and I'll tell you who you are. Apple or Android? Coke, Pepsi, or neither? BMW or Chevy? Brands are amazingly efficient and effective shorthands for richly detailed belief systems with which we either want to self-identify or outwardly reject. The brands we choose, wear, use, talk about, wish we could afford, avoid—they all represent aspects of who we are; what we believe, value, and trust; and how we want others to see us.

"Belief systems?" you wonder, raising an eyebrow. "Isn't a brand merely a signpost for the product or service itself?" Short answer: yes, if it's not a resilient brand. In the Conscience Economy, there will be no place for brands that don't sum up a set of relevant, inspiring beliefs. Even branded bleach. "But bleach is bleach," you retort. Well, what about a bleach brand that is highly vocal about protecting the groundwater supply and offers a more environmentally sensible means of disposal, is packaged sustainably, and demonstrates on its packaging and in its communications how killing germs fights disease, while its manufacturer actually supports and visibly helps to fight disease by supporting a range of health-related social enterprises? In effect, it's a bleach brand that engages with the Culture of Conscience.

After all, when we're given two similar options at a reasonably comparable price, we don't decide between products or services, we decide between brands. And when we make our choice, it's not because we like the signpost itself, it's because we value and align with all that it stands for, and increasingly, how it contributes to helping make the world as we'd like it to be.

The brands we like and want to be seen using are a means of identifying *ourselves*, our affiliation with others who like the same brand, our beliefs, what we value most. Brands are also who we work for and how we build our careers. A "good CV" is not only a history of the roles you've played; it's the quality and prestige of the brands for which you worked. Political parties, social movements, places, transportation solutions, exercise regimes—it's hard to think of a category of everyday life that isn't branded.

The proliferation of purchase choice is not the only reason strong branding should be foremost on the agenda for any organization today. The rise of a new set of purchase decision-making priorities makes it even more crucial. It is increasingly difficult to part with our money without at least a glancing consideration as to its impact on the wider world. "Every dollar you spend is a vote for something," proclaims a social entrepreneur, one of the founders of Project Provenance (provenance.it) an online marketplace that provides information transparency about new products, "so why not use that vote for something you believe in?"

Ignoring the consequences of our actions and purchases on the lives of others—and on the planet—will become harder and harder to do as real-time and contextually delivered information increasingly clarifies what those consequences are. It's like product labeling on steroids—except that the "ingredients" we'll see will be filtered to show what matters most to us, whether it's ethical production processes, the political biases and donation histories of executives, or the environmental and societal implications of a company's farms or factories. And the likelihood is, people will reject those products or services that are in some way contributing to issues they don't support.

And, of course, while we have more choice, we've never had less time to exercise it. We need shortcuts. In an increasingly chaotic and fluctuating business environment, brands will be ever more important navigation devices for us all. They will sum up all that we do to make the world better for everyone. They are more than our calling cards. They are the definition of who and what we are, and they are the building blocks of the world we want to bring into being. Your customers need you to make it easy for them to recognize that what they care about is inherent in your products, your services, and even your mode of operation. Building and managing a robust brand has never been more vital for success.

Put simply, to stand out, you have to stand for something. To stand out in the Conscience Economy, you must position your business and brand as an emblem of all that the emergent culture holds dear. Indeed, your brand is the most potent business asset you can manage, because it sums up, contains, and conveys all that you are and will be.

Brand Begins Within

Sadly, the word "brand" is one of the most misunderstood and misused words in business. Too often, it's thought of as what's on the outside. A mere skin. A logo, a color scheme, and some communications design guidance written up in a tidy document by people in the marketing department.

The misconception is somewhat forgivable, given the etymology of the term. Originally, as you no doubt know, branding *was* all about skin—cattle skin, to be precise. As variously owned business assets (cows) mingled on the plains, there had to be some way of identifying their owners.

The origin of the word is apt today. Products and services mingle on the plains of the global marketplace, and we need some way of knowing where they came from, to whom they belong, who produced them and how, and why we should adopt them into our lives.

What's more, we also need to know to whom *we* belong when we buy, invest in, or work for a brand. We don't just acquire the hard asset. We join the cult. We become a part of a group of like-minded people who are fans of the same brand. It's not dissimilar to being a fan of a particular sports team. There is a strong self-identification between people and the brands they love. In some cases, the careful discernment is as pragmatic as it is emotional, because once we're "in" the brand's ecosystem (hello, Apple) it can be hard to switch. Brands are a kind of mirror. We look for the reflection of our own values and dreams in the things that we buy.

Today, brands stand for how a product was produced, how the company operates, how it treats its people. Brands even stand for how a company positions itself with regard to politics. Pasta maker Barilla, for example, had an uncomfortable wake-up call when in 2013 its CEO made remarks perceived to be disparaging of same-sex relationships, triggering a mass boycott that swiftly went viral on social media.

Think about this for a moment. Because it's pretty astonishing. The political biases of a company executive—especially when they're perceived as extreme—can and do directly impact brand reputation, and consequently, sales, both positively and negatively. Brands like Chick-fil-A or television properties like *Duck Dynasty* have been battlegrounds for what we might call "conscience wars" between entrenched and polarized points of view on contemporary social issues.

Thus, powerful, magnetic branding is not what's on the surface. It's not decoration or dress-up. Those visually and aurally recognizable aspects of identity are merely brand signifiers. And when your company doesn't live up to the meaning that it signifies, people see right through it.

A strong brand starts deep within the business. It's more like the brain, the conscience of the organization. "Off brand" means wrong, "on brand" means right. If I may get a bit metaphysical or at least metaphorical, your brand is your company's soul.

Perhaps because the very concept of brand is somewhat abstract and conceptual, it's not unusual for it to be off-loaded to a creative team rather than discussed by all. To do so is a mistake. Because building and securing your brand by engaging all functions of the organization in the process, employing both left and right brains, is your company's most powerful way to reaffirm or rethink its purpose, future strategy, and market position.

In a brand-centric business, every decision is made based upon the values, intentions, and aspirations of the brand. And not by consulting a framework or manual, mind you. When the brand is continuously reinforced through rituals of company culture, and when everyone is continuously engaged in talking about and applying the brand to everyday work, it becomes internalized in each employee. To shamelessly misappropriate from Adam Smith, your brand can and should be the business's "invisible hand," steadily guiding innovation, daily operations, protocols, and conduct.

Conscientious Brands

As enlightenment becomes ever sexier, those brands that manifest socially and environmentally sensible ways of operating will be the winners. Why else would Walmart begin enforcing greener production standards in China, or Apple and the NFL put themselves on the front lines of a political debate about gay rights in Arizona? Today, the most overtly conscientious brands include "goodness-certified" products (green, Fair Trade, cruelty free, for example), handmade and artisanal products, ethical luxury, ethical fashion, hybrid automobiles, and one-for-one products. But they also include retailers that vocally support causes and put their money where their PR is, those with conscientious worker policies and conditions. In the U.K., the John Lewis Partnership, with its department stores and supermarkets, is thought of as more than big business or a stable of retail brands; it's a much-loved national institution, a cornerstone of British life, among those of all political persuasions.

What might the next set of brands dominating a new economy rooted in conscientiousness look like? How might we imagine new brands that are positioned to thrive and lead in a world where doing good matters as much as doing well?

Imagine if all the brands you used inspired you to be a better you in one way or another. What if, by choosing a particular product or service, you knew you were participating in progress in ways that are synchronized with your own values? The next wave of leading brands will be those that stand for a positive impact on humanity and the environment, in their own operations as well as through us, their buyers and users.

Every brand makes a promise. In the past, brands promised basic benefits like convenience, efficacy, style, speed, flavor, low cost, quality engineering, sex appeal, happiness, or luxury. Over time, and as technology has entered every aspect of our lives, brands have evolved to stand for more empowering personal capabilities like creativity, imagination, innovation, communication, playfulness, achievement, and collaboration.

Conscientious brands will take the evolution further. In the Conscience Economy, the brands people most value and love will...

- Make us not only smarter but wiser.
- Empower us to solve our toughest challenges.
- Enable us to help others grow.
- Help us be physically and emotionally healthy.
- Defend our physical, financial, and environmental safety.
- Heal rifts and conflicts.
- Enable us to fix, restore, and remake stuff.
- Protect us from overexposure.
- Help us disconnect from the chaos of life.
- Empower us to make the world more beautiful, fun, and friendly.
- Help us save energy and resources.
- Facilitate sharing.
- Bring us closer to nature.
- Guide us to places, things, and people that inspire us.
- Deepen our connections with no compromise of privacy.
- Bring out the best in humanity.

Old and New Basics

In the Conscience Economy, it is not only the brand promise that shifts. As people's expectations change, the basic principles for customer understanding and belief change, too. The old basics of rational and emotional benefits now include an overarching demand for personal agency, self and community empowerment, and positive social and environmental impact.

It's not enough to focus on what your product does or even how it makes someone feel for buying it. It is now equally essential to focus on where and how it was produced. For example, you no longer just buy a coffee. You buy a Rainforest Alliance–certified, organic, small-batch roasted, and custom-built pumpkin latte that's handcrafted and drizzled with caramel right in front of your eyes—at McDonald's. The provenance of the coffee beans makes us feel in the know, and the customization makes us feel special. Already, the production story behind a product—whether it's a cup of coffee, a microbrewed beer, or a sweater—is perhaps the most significant selling point among the international cohort of influential, young-minded, early-adopter customers who inhabit cities that lead the way for the mainstream, like San Francisco, Toronto, Barcelona, and even Beijing.

It's also no longer enough to instigate mere product desire. It's essential to invite a desire to participate in something bigger. For example, if you're an Apple fan, you don't just buy an iPhone. You join the hordes of other iPhone users around the world, signifying your membership in the cult of Apple. When you stack up its features and its build quality, it isn't necessarily the "best" in the smartphone category. The other people using it—the sense that they constitute a cohort that's in the know—is the real draw.

Here's a useful checklist list of old basics and new basics. Some of the shifts are subtle, others more dramatic. All are vital for business to understand and internalize, not only as marketing and communications principles but as drivers of value creation throughout your business. As you read the list, ask yourself: How can my business deliver on the new brand basics?

OLD BASIC	NEW BASIC
I know what it is	I know where and how it was produced
I know how effective it is	I know how much positive impact it makes
I'm smart for buying it	I'm making a difference by buying it
It makes me look good	It shows I'm in-the-know
I need to have it	I need to be a part of it
It communicates with a sense of humor	It enables me to share my sense of humor
It's politically and socially neutral	It heroically represents my point of view
It helps make my life easier	It gives me power to change my life and world

The New Brand Management

In the Conscience Economy, brand management is the vital wellspring of value creation because it is the manifestation of belief converted into action. But everyone—not just customer-facing staff—is responsible for its delivery. When such a core prerogative is relegated to a single functional department, its effectiveness is diminished. Start by acknowledging and communicating that brand management is part of everyone's job.

If this sounds like breezy rhetoric, consider these questions: How can the team responsible for strategic acquisitions scan the marketplace for appropriate prospects if they haven't internalized the ultimate ambition of the brand? How can engineers create new solutions if they don't have a personal sense of where the business is going, and why it's going there? How does HR establish coherent hiring standards that ensure not only the attraction of talent, but also cultural fit, if it isn't directly engaged in the brand? Indeed, if your brand is not meaningful to everyone, as well as applicable to each employee's daily work and decision making, then you've got an alignment problem. Fortunately, in my experience, the vast majority of people absolutely love getting involved in the creation, augmentation, evolution, and renewal of the brands for which they work. It can be the most exciting and meaningful part of their work. I've even gotten to know software engineers who became their companies' most outspoken advocates.

This is not to say you should disband or laterally distribute your brand team, though it's smart to assign a brand steward—a senior leader—in every function. That includes supply chain and logistics, legal, finance, facilities, HR, and more. Most crucial is to elevate the brand stewardship mandate. Reporting relationships are one way to do this. Consider making design, product innovation, communications, sales, and marketing all directly accountable to brand leadership; after all, these are the functions most tasked with value creation and delivery, communication, insight and foresight, creativity, and interaction with customers.

But before you shuffle your org chart, start by clarifying strategic roles and objectives. Key responsibilities need to be assigned:

- Leading and stewarding the process of creating a meaningful and thriving brand
- Aligning corporate behavior, operations, strategy, and decision making around brand
- Translating brand into new products, effective communication, and frontline sales strategy

- Maintaining consistent and recognizable brand standards that properly signify all that the business stands for in the broader marketplace

However you choose to organize it, the processes I describe below *must* involve participation across multiple functions, job roles, and layers in the business. It's okay to look outside the company for help facilitating and distilling the meaning you create, but the content and meaning you generate *must* come from within. The process is as persuasive and aligning as the outcome.

1. Connect Your Values with Your Strategy

Ah, core values. So much good intent, and so many business books extolling the business value of core values. Does the following scenario sound familiar? A company workshops a set of core values, feels great about them, attributes them in some way to Our Great Founder from years past, and posts them somewhere on the corporate website. Sometimes they're carved in sandstone at corporate HQ. They pop up in speeches from time to time. And other than that, values can sadly simply be a check in the box. "Yup, mission and values, we did those a few years ago at the offsite." As for the values themselves, they're always lofty and hard to argue with, and they can be pretty similar from company to company. "Respect" is a common one. "Integrity" is another. Even banks—currently the least trusted of business sectors when it comes to integrity—use this lofty language in their online "mission statements."

The problem is that it's all too rare that a business connects its values with its brand, let alone its strategy. But your brand *is* your values and your strategy. It is everything that you are. And it's actually possible—thrilling, even—to make the link.

In the Conscience Economy, it's vital to make this link because business operates in a culture in which values drive everything. I won't be the first to say it: your values need to inform everything you do, not just sit on the intranet. The chief creative officer of an agency where I once worked even had the company's values tattooed on his arm so he'd never forget them. I'm not one to argue with passion, and his was considerable.

Fifteen years ago, while I was working at an innovation consultancy in San Francisco, one of our clients, UPS, asked us if we could help them build a strategic framework that they could use to connect their legacy and their core values with their future vision and strategy.

My colleague Erika Gregory and I invented a framework and process to address the challenge, and I've been using it ever since, with organizations across a range of sectors, from telecom networking and consumer electronics to professional services and even public sector community groups. We call it the Brand Charter.

The Brand Charter is particularly effective as a sorting and prioritizing tool because it helps groups organize different ideas and ingredients of the company's beliefs, goals, and plans.

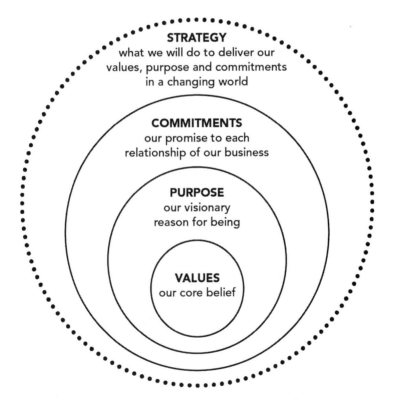

The charter is based on the principle of layering. Imagine a sphere, like the earth, with a deep gravitational pull toward its core, and dynamic life and interaction at its surface. This sphere—which is the totality of your brand—is composed of a series of layers of meaning, almost like a Russian nesting doll, with each layer encircling and protecting the layers within it.

At the core of a brand identity are an organization's **values** and beliefs. Imagine those values and beliefs inhabiting a sphere at the core of a larger entity. These are things that will never change. The business model, the product line, the headquarters, the board—these might all go through multiple alterations. But those truths that are, within your business, sacrosanct and held to be self-evident, to quote the U.S. Declaration of Independence, these must never change. This is where conscientious brand building begins.

The next layer out, the sphere in which your core values are nested, is the organization's **purpose**. It's your reason for being, beyond just making money. It's often best summed up in a single sentence, but again, the most important thing is not the perfect sentence, it's the clarity of the idea. This is the place to be wildly ambitious and visionary, to lay out a proclamation of intent that's groundbreaking, life improving, planet healing. There is no reason to hold back or aim for some kind of short-term realism. Spread happiness to all corners of the earth. Connect billions everywhere to a free education. Eliminate late diagnoses of disease. Banish pain and suffering. Increase human lifespans. Give every newborn baby an equal shot at life.

The next layer out from purpose is the organization's **commitments** to each of those categories of people with whom it interacts. Its commitment to employees, suppliers, customers, citizens, partners, and more. This is often a series of up to nine different statements—it could indeed comprise more, but it's best to limit the types of relationships to a manageable number.

And the final layer on the "outside" of this sphere we are creating is **strategy**—what the organization will actually do to manifest all the layers within, how you will deliver on your commitments. Strategy is the market-facing, public-facing layer of the overall brand charter. It is the one component of the framework that does change, as the external operating environment—disruptive technologies, emergent behaviors, customer demands, and other external factors—changes. Strategy articulates how you will mitigate risk and seize opportunity. And strategy is informed from two directions—from both outside the enterprise and simultaneously from within. In other words, although strategy is the organization's response to market conditions, it is simultaneously supported by and even fueled by all that is encircled within the framework—it directly expresses the commitments to each business relationship, it delivers on the organizational purpose, and it is the means by which the organization's core values are delivered and made real in the world.

But the world changes, constantly. The continual flux in which business needs to operate requires that strategy be revisited on a regular basis and summed up within this structure.

From years of experience deploying different frameworks in a range of boardrooms, I've concluded that this particular structure is, above all else, highly effective as a "sorting" mechanism that brings clarity and cohesion to a diverse set of agendas and priorities. If, for example, a team feels that "sustainability" is something important to the organization, we can then discuss: Is sustainability a core value, is it the purpose of the organization, is it actually a commitment to some key stakeholders, or is it a strategy to address an urgent need? I bring up sustainability intentionally, as it often emerges in these conversations, but it never "lands" in the same place within this framework.

I caution you to avoid the trap of wordsmithing. It can take weeks, months, to agree on the particulars of language, and even after years of working internationally, I can still be caught off guard by how one word can mean such different things to different people. For example, I've worked with a leadership team who couldn't agree on the meaning of the word "progress." To me, the word is irrefutably positive, referring to significant steps forward for humanity. But there were a few executives who saw the word in a negative light, who believed it suggested a kind of plodding incrementalism. My point is, important truths are always *ideas*, not terms, and while it's helpful as a memory aid to sum these truths up with single words, it always takes more than one word to get the richness, depth, and distinctiveness of an idea across.

2. Make Brand a Story

Frameworks are great for helping groups discuss, sort, and organize ideas. They're particularly excellent for demonstrating relational connections. But let's admit it: no framework ever got your pulse racing. Frameworks don't change hearts and minds—or behaviors. Stories do.

Here's a simple exercise to get your team familiar with the concept. Ask each of them to describe Santa Claus in their own words. I (and you) already know what you'll hear.

Every story will be told differently. Different words, different story structure. Each person's story will be unique and personal, but everyone will describe the same persona, the same intention, the same rituals, the same identity signifiers. No one will struggle to remember the basic narrative. No mnemonic device or framework will be required. You'll hear just a simple story, usually peppered with fondly remembered anecdotes from real life.

Next, ask if this "person" they are describing is real. Again, different stories, same meaning: "He's a spirit of generosity, we're all a little bit Santa at Christmas." "He's magical when kids need magic in their lives, and we want them to believe in him as long as possible." "He's kind of a ritual and we all play along because it brings joy and happiness and fun into our home." "Of course he's real. He's in all of us."

Santa is exactly like a brand. Because a brand is a recognizable identity, a belief system, a personality, and most importantly, today, a set of recognizable behaviors. We know he lives at the North Pole, that he has a team of elves making toys, and that he knows whether children have been bad or good. We know he's chubby, has a big white beard, and wears a red suit trimmed in white fur. (That's the Coca-Cola contribution. He looks like a big can of Coke.) We know how he sounds (ho ho ho) and we know that he comes down our chimney to put presents under the tree and into our stockings. We know that he's omniscient but kind. And we know that he's really a spirit or an idea that we try to embody for the children in our lives each Christmas. Even non-Christians know of Santa Claus. We see his image everywhere.

And a great brand is inspiring, just as Santa is. Meanwhile, religious associations aside, Santa (who has become a true pagan in his old age anyway) is an object lesson in what I call story management. He evolved organically, and yet the word and image have spread so consistently that people from various backgrounds and points of view can describe him accurately. Not only what he looks like and what he does, but his spirit, too.

It's not important whether everyone in your business can recite your brand charter. What matters is that they can tell, in their own words, a

"Santa Claus Story" about your company and brand. The point is to get outside of the traditional technique of creating a brand framework with specific words. The ultimate objective in conscientious brand management is for everyone in the organization to be able to tell the story of what the company is about—what it stands for, where it's going, and most importantly, why—in their own words. It's immediately evident whether people are telling the same story.

In other words, if everyone can share a personalized story of your business and what it means with the same consistency that we all can describe Santa Claus, then bravo, you've got a foundation for contemporary brand management in place.

How do you get there? You might already be closer than you think. Start by asking your people to tell, in two minutes, why they work for the business and what they believe the brand stands for. Suggest that they include their thoughts about how the brand is impacting the world. Note how consistently, or inconsistently, they tell their stories. Are their words personal? Do they include an anecdote? Are they reciting language from a training session? Just listen, and notice what you hear. It's likely that you'll be amazed at the consistency. But here's a hedge: if the responses are profoundly misaligned (in my experience, they never have been), then your job is to listen at least for recognizable patterns, for themes that appear throughout the stories. The goal here is not to assess whether people are telling the same story in the same way, nor is it to convince them to do so. You're looking for commonality that you can use to link points of view.

Next, model the act of storytelling yourself. Because the most powerful thing you can do as a leader is tell the story as you feel it and understand it. Doing this gives permission for others to personalize the way they talk about—and put to work—the values, purpose, commitments, and strategy of the company.

In the rare instance where people are unable to describe their own relationship to the company and its purpose in any kind of linked or consistent way, you will need to reinforce the importance of brand, and then demonstrate (from leadership as well as from customers) a few examples of consistent meaning shared in diverse ways. Divergent stories will quickly coalesce, because it is natural for people, and especially employees, to want to belong to something. If people don't have a story about your brand within them, they will want one, and will be open to receiving and personalizing it.

For stories to spread, they have to be told, reinforced, discussed, and at times, ritualized. A great brand gets energy and potency from being at the heart of everyday conversations across the company. The more transparently you include your brand story as a driver of your leadership decisions, the more your people will put your story to work. In time, telling the story, and putting its meaning to work in everyday business decisions, becomes habitual.

3. Establish "Consistency Guidelines"

To state the obvious, brand value does not rise or fall based upon colors, typefaces, or photographic style guidelines. But it can rise and fall based upon consistency. So traditional brand guidelines (typically packaged in a "brand book") really matter, and they need rigorous enforcement and advocacy from the top down and the bottom up. Consistency is vital.

Without consistency, you're unrecognizable. Imagine if every time you saw your partner, he (or she) had undergone plastic surgery and had a different face. Imagine if he had a different voice too. Would you treat him the same way you did yesterday? Would you even engage with him? You couldn't do it. Because you need to recognize the person with whom you're in a relationship of trust and value exchange.

Okay, that's an extreme example. But I hope it sticks in your mind, because multisensory identity guidelines are crucial. Calling them brand guidelines relegates them to a communications design function. Start calling them consistency guidelines.

Multisensory design consistency is as professionalized as financial accounting, and every business should take it just as seriously. Arguably, design consistency was as much a driver of Apple's meteoric resurrection as the experiential innovation that fueled Apple's portfolio. Suffice it to say, consistent and coherent logo use, colors, typeface, photographic and illustration style, sound components, real-world materials, and architectural and design principles are all as important as they've ever been. But here's what's new: a playful spirit and a willingness to let consumers manipulate and experiment with your identity are also vital components for brand expression. Showing your willingness to break your own rules from time to time keeps your identity vibrant, surprising, and human. Witness Google's continual manipulation of its brand mark, a powerful way of stating the company's point of view on current events.

Your brand is not only your identity but the voice with which you speak. Tone is crucial. With the premium they place on breaking down hierarchies and peer-to-peer connection, denizens of the Conscience Economy expect that brands speak as peers too, not condescendingly or patronizingly. The invitation to do good must be more like a seduction. Political correctness is the enemy of the Conscience Economy. Too often, consumers associate "responsible" with uncomfortable.

For example, a London advertising agency I know was recently hired to reposition and create a campaign for recycled toilet paper. I know what you're thinking: scratchy. As Gail, the agency's CEO, put it to me over a conversation in an editing suite, "No amount of sustainability is worth a scratchy bathroom experience. But repositioned as 'ethical luxury,' it offers a more compelling proposition. Because people actually do want to do something good. They just don't want to pay more for it, or suffer for it."

Gail's observation is backed up by empirical evidence that may seem at odds with the motivations driving the Conscience Economy. Research shows that, although people increasingly care about social and environmental issues, most are unwilling to make sacrifices in order to support them, at least in their purchasing habits. I jump on Skype with Giana Eckhardt, one of the authors of *The Myth of the Ethical Consumer,* to get a better understanding of this paradox. And she puts it to me straight: when it comes to the mainstream, "when they're spending money, people still care about value and convenience."

Giana explains that the marketplace has unintentionally trained us to assume that products and services that are overtly marketed to us with a social or environmental purpose are more expensive, even when they're not. So an overt social or environmental message can imply added expense and subconsciously put off customers even though they care about the topical benefits being conveyed. The exception to the perception of added cost as compromise, Giana notes, are people (aka hipsters) with, as she puts it, "identity concerns," who want to be seen as caring and conscientious. For them, making an overtly conscientious purchase—signified by a desirable brand—indicates their social status, and they're more than willing to pay for it. And when early adopters adopt a brand, it gains that ineffable cool factor, which can ultimately spread to the mainstream. Hence, I realize, the win-win of ethically luxurious toilet paper that feels as good on the conscience as it does, um, elsewhere.

Dismantling the notion that "good" means compromise is key to the Conscience Economy. Good can feel great, be naughty, wink-wink at you, or offer an experience that even feels indulgent. Indeed, the smartest brands in the Conscience Economy will be those with a voice and personality that is authentic, friendly, human, witty, and even darkly ironic. No one likes self-righteousness.

Staying on Top

A healthy brand is like a vibrant beating heart. In tough times, in many categories, particularly fast moving consumer goods, people will forgo their ideal brand to save money. The less cash people have the more price is going to motivate them. However, your competition will be playing the pricing game too. That downward pricing spiral can be deadly. Brands with enough equity can weather these storms of economic uncertainty.

If you're currently enjoying your position at the top of the brand value charts, I have a special message for you. I worked with one of the world's most valuable brands for several years. When sales were good, the brand was strong. Very little attention was paid to keeping it that way; indeed, the company ceased to manage the brand as an asset. It didn't even have a CMO. And when sales began to decline, the brand declined, fatally. This is because the organization stopped internalizing future trends and believing it should change. It took its brand strength for granted in the good times, and neglected to future-proof it against unforeseen disruption. This is one of the most dangerous slippery slopes a successful company can face. When things are good, brand metrics appear strong, and the tendency is to maintain current procedures, to vigorously defend a status quo that's driving seemingly endless profit, and to neglect the management of brand meaning as a core asset.

But if the brand has not been future-proofed for change, and the relationships with all those who are engaged in the brand itself are not open channels for dialogue, there may well be unseen vulnerability. "Only the paranoid survive," goes the famous Andy Grove quote. Never take your brand health for granted. Treat it as your most vital asset, and nurture it appropriately.

With a healthy, vibrant, meaningful brand as your North Star, your compass, your guiding force for ongoing adaptation to the changing world around you, you future-proof yourself against the inevitable disruptions that buffet every business.

In the Conscience Economy the most robust meaning you can create—and the most powerful brand position you can secure in the hearts and minds of not only your customers but all the people your business touches—is that of a brand that stands for something authentically, socially, environmentally, humanly good. But the brand must also deliver on that promise. It's no longer about compartmentalizing values, purpose, promise, and strategy. It's about integrating them. It's no longer about departmentalizing corporate social responsibility. It's about embedding positive impact in everything you do.

5

The Death of CSR

A few years ago it was frequently said that business[people] ought to acquire a 'social consciousness.' What was usually meant was that business[people] were responsible for the consequences of their actions in a sphere somewhat wider than that covered by their profit-and-loss statements. Do you think that business[people] should recognize such responsibilities and do their best to fulfill them?

Yes: 95.5 percent
No: 1.6 percent
Depends: 4.7 percent
Don't Know: 0.2 percent

—*Fortune*, March 1946

A year after the end of the worst global conflict in history, *Fortune* magazine polled business executives (who, in a manner so charmingly indicative of the times, were called businessmen) on their responsibilities beyond profit making. Other than the term businessmen, the question—and the answers—are surprisingly contemporary.

In a spirit of digitally enabled appropriation, I took just a teeny bit of millennial liberty with the wording—replacing "men" with "people"—so you could experience the date of its publication as a kind of punch line. Gender equality might still not reign in the boardroom, but the fact that "businessmen" is an utterly outdated term is evidence that things have progressed significantly on the social front since this survey. What's fascinating here is that in a business era even more overtly sexist than the butt-pinching business culture of *Mad Men,* that as cigarette smoke wafted through corner offices and gamine secretaries pecked away at typewriters, a humane and socially progressive sentiment was taking hold among the business majority. This notion of social stewardship accompanied a growing sense that corporations were very much public institutions, not unlike universities, or government itself. Even back in 1946, business was beginning to feel culturally sanctioned to take wider responsibility in society beyond generating profit.

Baked In

Fast-forward to the next millennium. It's another sunbaked Friday in East L.A., and I've just walked into Intelligentsia Coffee, a classic example of a third space hangout in one of the more stylishly pseudo-scruffy parts of town. "Third space," as you no doubt know, is a term for that unique category of place that's neither home nor office—a place that has the comfort of the former with the social productivity and fast Wi-Fi of the latter. In typical third space style, the café is full of young, creative-looking tweeters with their iPads, carefully maintained beards, piercings, tattoos, and ironic tee shirts. The air is thick with the nutty-warm scent of coffee, brewed masterfully, of course, by skinny youths who, based on their caffeinated chatter, seem to have gotten dual master's degrees in barista management and cognitive theory.

It's all very poetic, and for someone of my generation, perhaps a bit "been-there-before"—but a closer look reveals some emergent trends in action. And before you argue that what I'm describing is merely the marginal and rarified environs of a major cultural capital, and not the province of the ordinary Jane and Joe, do remember where trends begin. After all, L.A. is the dream factory, and its workers, its creative class, are clustered around this very neighborhood, with its interesting bookshops, artisanally produced soaps scented with trail-foraged evergreen boughs, and vintage-decorated grunge bars. Unlike Vegas, what happens here *doesn't* stay here. It migrates. To everywhere else.

So I have a look around. And right there, on a shelf next to the cash register, I see something so perfectly of the moment that I do a double take. In a new row evocative of a miniature Donald Judd sculpture, sit three tastefully designed boxes of energy bars, carefully and lovingly merchandised like design objects. On each bar, in big, bold, sans serif type: "THIS BAR SAVES LIVES."

I always like branding that gets to the point. And indeed, this particular product falls into the category of buy-to-donate. For every bar you buy, the company's nonprofit partner gives a donation. The product itself doesn't save lives—the for-profit manufacturer of the product supports a nonprofit that has created another product that feeds malnourished children in Africa.

The intentions are great. And the business and the earnestness of its founders are emblematic of the moment. But can This Bar Saves Lives become a leading brand?

The buy-one-give-one model can be tough to support, as I learned from Duncan Goose, who started the brand One a decade ago in the United Kingdom. Buy something, support something. Duncan is a pioneer in conscientious brand building. After spending a few years in the international advertising industry in London, Duncan decided at the ripe old age of twenty-eight that he had learned all that business could teach him, and that it was time to get schooled by life itself in the wider world. He quit his plush job, sold everything he had, and embarked on a round-the-world motorcycle trip that in and of itself is worthy of a major motion picture.

It was an amazing and dangerous adventure. He almost lost his eyesight after hitting a deer in Alberta, Canada. He was shot at in Mexico. He narrowly avoided being kidnapped on the Afghan border. But the most extraordinary experience he described was being in Honduras and surviving the strongest hurricane to ever hit its shores.

The coast was literally decimated. The entire infrastructure disappeared in a matter of hours. While riding along what looked like a beach full of rubble, he came to realize it had been a village. "There was a single structure that looked like a bandstand, you know, all open to the air. A woman was sitting in it. I rode up to her. She told me this was her village, and this structure had been her home." Duncan was astonished. But nothing prepared him for what happened next. She asked if he had a place to stay, and when he shook his head, she led him to a nearby refugee camp where he immediately became accepted into the community.

"People who have nothing will share with you what they have," he recalls, and his eyes immediately fill with tears. "I had the means to purify water, but I was still given water by the chief of the community. I was feeling so…" he trails off, and he chokes up. His eyes are shining with tears. I'm silent. I can see that this particular experience was a life-changing one that still sustains him.

There was no access to electricity, no fresh water. Duncan experienced firsthand the preciousness of what, for most of us, in the U.K. and the U.S. at least, is a commodity so common that we have a porcelain fountain in the middle of our homes, replenished at the touch of a lever with gushing potable water. But instead of drinking this abundance, we—well, to put it bluntly—we pee and poop into it. The day is coming when this will seem as surreal and wasteful as throwing gold into a sacred lake.

Duncan stayed with the community for a while. He spent a day digging a house out of a mudslide. He joined forces with some tourists from Switzerland and Belgium and somehow managed to raise about $100,000 to help the community. Eventually he moved on to more adventures, and ultimately back to London, where the lesson stayed with him.

The bottled water category is highly competitive, but innovation in the water category, he explained to me, is "about as exciting as changing the cap." So one night in a pub with friends, Duncan decided there was an opportunity to be creative at the intersection of the water sector and public health in countries where safe drinking water was scarce. The One Water brand was born, to an FMCG product company where a social sensibility is baked in to the very business model itself.

The drumbeat of "we executives/investors/managers/employees have a wider role to play in society" may feel fashionably of the moment in today's more relaxed and open-collar boardrooms, but in fact, the debate about the role of business in society—and whether it should assume the obligation to give back to the community in which it operates—is well over a century old. Admittedly, the "C" in the term CSR came a while later. But social responsibility has been on the discussion agenda as long as the balance sheet has, as we are about to see.

Business and Society: The Dance Begins

Indeed, the history of what we now call CSR is the history of business itself, something we don't obviously have time to cover in this chapter.

Nevertheless, there is fascinating historical evidence that illustrates how the demands of business and the needs of society have been entangled in an elaborate and evolving pas de deux since the dawn of the corporation. Enlightened industrialists (like the Quaker-run enterprises in Victorian Great Britain) recognized from the get-go that they needed to provide support for the health and well-being of their workforce, whether directly through housing and other essential resources, or through philanthropic support of public institutions. Sometimes seen as separate forces, and other times viewed as integrated domains, the practices of business and the well-being of society have always been dependent upon one another, because healthy workers, thriving resources, and a stable customer base are the core components of business itself.

CSR as an exercise and a service manifests the most beautiful of human intentions—it's been essential in the evolution of our civilization. As a discipline and a catalyst, I love it to death. But it's served its purpose. It's time to offer the function a graceful retirement, hand it a gold watch, and move on.

Oh no, I'm not talking about retiring the CSR *team*! On the contrary. These fervent and visionary people need to stick it out and step up, because they have far more important work to do. They need to get out of their specialized, professionalized department and make an even bigger difference in the enterprise and the world. They are, indeed, the next COOs, the next CMOs, and the next CEOs, the next congressional representatives, the new leaders. The CSR team are steeped in factual and anecdotal knowledge that's needed for the Conscience Economy to take flight.

But before we take off for the future, let's have a look at the runway. Because although massive change really does happen overnight, the run-up can take far longer. And in the case of the Conscience Economy, it's been decades of trial and error, with a major disaster partway through, that's led to this moment. For your delectation, as well as your use as a provocative topic of discussion during a lull at your next business dinner, I offer a brief history of how the advancement of CSR from a debate to a management function unfolded.

To whom is the corporation ultimately responsible? This, perhaps, is the central question. People's essential humanity hasn't grown, it's not like we've evolved—but what's happened is that we know more, we experience more.

The whole thing really kicked off during the Industrial Revolution, when industrialized manufacturing and distribution on a mass scale heretofore never seen, gave rise to a host of dilemmas, from the emergence of inhumane working conditions in factories and mines to intensified urban pollution as hordes of laborers moved from the countryside to dense conurbations of manufacturing. The "dark Satanic Mills" of William Blake's nineteenth-century poem began spreading across the landscape, producing goods efficiently but belching smoke and soot into the air while in too many cases, harboring suffering workers within. Essayists and novelists, as writers do, critiqued the consequences of the explosive growth of the time. And occasionally, some semblance of legal policy contravened. Briefly, in the later 1800s, it was actually a requirement to provide evidence of social usefulness in order to receive a governmental charter of incorporation.

But by the end of the Civil War, with the U.S. desperate to kick-start the economy again, nearly any business was granted its incorporation documents. And within a few years, corporations had grown exponentially stronger and more powerful. An era of nearly unchecked corporate irresponsibility bellowed forth.

Collapse Causes Conscience

Thank goodness for the Great Depression. Without the cataclysmic and near-total collapse of the financial system, say business historians, the nascent dialogue about the public, social, and environmental role of business might have disappeared forever. The business ecosystem itself had to be rebuilt, and in that process, ideas about a broader role for business ethics and governance in the greater community reclaimed a place in the discourse.

As corporate structures and governance evolved, and as citizens' and social awareness increased, the conversation shape-shifted. And although it has not been linear, looking back, it's not hard to conclude that there were clear phases through which discussion and the culture have moved.

Particularly useful, I think, is the series of themed phases that were described by Patrick Murphy, writing in the *University of Michigan Business Review* in 1978. Although these "eras" don't have absolute beginning and end dates (does any era?) they still, even today, elegantly express an evolving sensibility of business in relationship with society through the decades.

Murphy suggests that a more formalized reciprocity between business and society began in what he calls a *philanthropic era*. This rather long period of business history can be both defined (and limited) by the singularly predominant strategy of the business donating a portion of its proceeds to causes in the community. It seems that the impulse toward philanthropy was driven then, as it still is today, by a combination of personal commitment or experience and a wish to improve community relations.

For example, as early as 1875, the accounting books of New York City store R. H. Macy's show that the company was contributing to an orphan asylum—an expression of Macy's personal interest in nurturing a positive relationship with the urban community from which his customers and his employees came.

Robber barons like Vanderbilt and Carnegie, looking for a permanent legacy, endowed universities, art museums, and other institutions, establishing their names as heroic and aristocratic noblesse oblige enablers of social betterment. Given that those who had amassed sufficient wealth to build a world-class university had likely done it at the expense of those who were exploited by their near-limitless powers, the desire to recast their celebrity and rebrand the meaning of their own names makes perfect sense. It was as savvy as any other decision they made, and perhaps the benefits of their giving in the long term outweigh the means by which they became capable of doing it. A strange variant on the Robin Hood theme— steal from everyone, then give (some of it) back to everyone.

Recently, I was at the Frieze Art Fair, a contemporary art trade show that fairly crawls with high-net-worth individuals (I'm not one of them) ready to throw down six figures or more for a "picture." I ended up chatting with a real estate financier from New York City who ranted passionately to me about how he resents "named giving." For him, the truest motivation for donating to important causes should be the impact it makes, not celebrity or narcissistic self-glorification. His point of view is provocative. Does the motivation matter if the giving happens anyway? Is the "amass great wealth, then give some of it back" model really viable in the long term? One argument in favor of traditional philanthropy is that the "who gives more" status competition encourages generosity.

On the other hand, the current system, both socially and economically, keeps many institutions and particularly charities locked in an ongoing dependence on donations, on aid, when perhaps positive impact and innovation to solve societal and environmental problems could instead be a more daily economic, personal, and business imperative and thus in the long term, more sustainable.

Another form of philanthropy is blurrier in terms of its deepest motivations. For example, records show that in this same so-called philanthropic era, during the late 1800s, National Cash Register initiated a number of what look like rather visionary employee welfare methods that wouldn't seem out of place in the Googleplex. The company provided medical facilities, bathhouses, and lunchrooms for employees. This was seen at the time, as Google's own employee benefits and environments are today, as a mix of humane empathy and sheer business savvy. Healthy, well-fed employees are also more productive employees.

Today, you can't say YMCA to a certain generation without a slightly embarrassed recollection of the karaoke rendition of the Village People hit. Everyone loves the exuberance and spirit of the song, but the kitsch connotation doesn't do the actual organization justice. The YMCA was one of the earliest pioneers of social responsibility, and one of the first to have a meaningful intersection with business.

Founded in the U.K. in 1844 and eventually spreading to the U.S., the YMCA was radical in its time, and in some ways its founding mission still feels contemporary today. Created to support the strengthening of mind, body, and spirit (hence the three-sided logo in the familiar logotype) the YMCA, and later the YWCA, provided a safe haven and accommodation for rural young men and women moving to the city. By World War I, businesses like railroad companies were supporting the organizations with funding. Again, the motivation was a mix of humanitarian and practical concerns—the YMCA provided safety and accommodation for their workers.

According to Murphy, the philanthropic era lasted well into the 1950s. And it should be noted that, although corporate philanthropy continues, and indeed most major charities couldn't exist without it, it cannot be taken for granted. Donating a portion of operating costs or potential shareholder return to charities opens up governance challenges that have long been debated in the courts as well as the boardrooms.

The central question—should businesses be giving shareholder dollars away?—is perhaps moot today because of the broad shift in our sensibilities, but it took nearly a century of practice before the dust settled on the argument.

Increasing Awareness

Philanthropy is a theme we will return to later, because it too is evolving. For now, on with our runway. Sometime in the 1950s, Murphy's next era came into being. In the *awareness era,* the enterprise begins to acknowledge and identify areas where business needs to engage more fully. We see the genesis in the *Fortune* poll. It makes sense that, as the world began to rebuild after the mass destruction brought about by World War II, business would begin to see itself as more than a mere participant in civilization. Business could be the engine of growth, health, even justice—albeit still largely through philanthropic giving and employee welfare. But by the 1950s, academics and management experts were writing articles with CSR in their titles.

By the late 1960s, and current with the climax of the civil rights movement, the *issues era* arose. Businesses began believing that they could and should participate in tackling specific issues—for example, urban decay, pollution, and environmental and geopolitical dilemmas. However, throughout the sixties, it was still more talk than action—and executionally, business continued to focus on corporate philanthropy and, when essential, community relations, to assuage its sense that it had more to do than make money. The debate over the role of business in society still had no clear winner.

Despite this, in the late '70s something different started to happen. The *responsiveness era* arose, from about 1978 onward. And this is the period when what is now officially called corporate social responsibility became a part of the strategic management of the business. Worker conditions were taken more seriously, and policies regarding diversity and ecology began to be addressed more directly. By the '80s, there was a clearly identifiable—and impactful—shift from talk to action.

Although there had been a century of debate, experimentation, media, and academic theorizing, this is the period that most people will tell you saw the actual birth of CSR. The reason for this, I think, is because it's when the intention became categorized, professionalized, and integrated into strategic management.

Professionalized Corporate Citizenship

At last, after more than a century of dialogue and good intention, the moment arrives when the CSR we know, love, or reject as lip service emerges into corporate life. I'm intrigued by this *responsiveness era*, one that practitioners describe with the kind of reverence that architects and Italophiles reserve for the Renaissance, and I decide I need to talk to some people who were there. I'm skeptical about the field and its future, and this is perhaps a provocative point of view given that CSR is so well-intentioned. I want to learn more about what it was like when it started from someone who will share an unvarnished and firsthand point of view. But where would I find such a person? It occurs to me that if I call one of the many consultancies that serve CSR departments, I'd get at best one-sided hopefulness, at worst beaten-down-but-still-faithful defensiveness.

I'd been working with a group of executive MBA students at the Cambridge Judge Business School, which positions itself as a premier institution preparing future business leaders for success in the Conscience Economy. In other words, the perfect environment for exploring not only the history of the field, but the dimensions of its current space as well as its future.

While working on the project, I learn that a member of the program's administration, Jane, had worked for a pioneering organization called Business in the Community, one of the U.K.'s first organizations founded to bring business and communities together to solve challenging social and urban issues. I hear from my research team that Jane has a strong point of view on the topic.

I take the train from London to Cambridge. Jane is a fount of energy, the kind of person who seems to hover a few inches off the ground. We meet over lunch at a café just across from the Gothic spires of King's College. The discussion takes off so quickly that we forget to order. (Later, I have a sandwich on the train back to London.)

There's something intriguing about a person making the decision to work in a field that hasn't fully formed yet. It strikes me as either bold or, given the context and meaning of social responsibility, perhaps motivated by something deeper. So, I dive right in and I ask her how she ended up involved in a field that hadn't quite taken shape.

At first she's reluctant to give the whole story. "It's very personal," she explains with classic British reserve. "I'm American," I answer with a small grin. "We love oversharing."

And that's when Jane explains how at the dawn of the '80s she had been working for one of the Big 5 consultancies (there were five back then). As Jane puts it, "Even they didn't know what to do with me." I can almost imagine why: this woman is anything but left-brained. While she was away on holiday, a sudden family tragedy occurred. Grief, and deep questions about the meaning of work and life, triggered her decision to abandon the corporate world and do some soul seeking. She traveled to the most alien and spiritually sustaining place she could imagine: the Himalayas.

As emotionally motivated pilgrimages often do, her journey stretched into weeks, and when she returned she decided she wanted more meaning in her work life, perhaps by working in development in emerging markets. Given her credentials, she found a position as a temp for the local director of Amnesty International. Before long she was recruited by an organization called Business in the Community, where she worked for seven years.

As she puts it, "It was serendipitous luck. I didn't need to turn my back on my business experience. I didn't need to work in developing markets. There were issues to be dealt with right here in my own country."

The U.K. was ahead of the game, as it turns out. After a series of riots—in Liverpool and in Brixton—a group of concerned business leaders set up Business in the Community to directly address urban social challenges.

There was a mantra behind the organization: "healthy high streets need healthy back streets." This is a very British expression—translated into American English, it might be "healthy business districts need healthy residential districts." This sounds as eminently practical today as it was visionary then. And it's the genesis of a principle that will come to govern the way we all make business decisions in the future.

When the social fabric of a community has broken down, particularly in economically deprived areas, someone needs to fix it. Not only for stability and safety, but for a sustainable community. And for business. Without healthy, happy residents, where's the healthy, happy employee base? Where are the customers? Managers?

And so, at the very beginning, BITC took the lead in tackling very real, local, urban issues. It built links between businesses and communities, persuading companies to get involved—for example, in supporting small businesses, offering training programs for unemployed youth, and participating in literacy programs in schools. The organizations gave people and time as much as money and resources, and perhaps more significantly, the effort introduced a generation of business executives to the pressing social issues that were literally within a few streets of their shining headquarters.

Again, although the intentions were good, the reality was that companies saw this kind of social interaction as an extra rather than fundamental to their operations. But the potential for greater business and social reciprocity was now firmly on the radar. BITC built a conduit between enterprise and community organizations.

Despite the excellence of the work of BITC, and its impressive roster of charter members, the organization struggled to expand serious, committed community involvement beyond thirty or so path-finding companies. Many BITC members still viewed it as part of their charity mission, and at the time it was tough to get most companies to significantly increase their individual contributions. After years of building and nurturing collaborative relationships between businesses and community organizations, Jane ultimately found it frustrating that many companies were unwilling to get more deeply involved in what is still a compelling and urgent mission.

I ask Jane what she thinks of CSR now. "It's become segmented and professionalized," she answers with a wry smile, pointing out that it even has professional qualifications. "It's a mature product. If it were a product line, this is what you'd expect it to be, thirty years on. You'd expect it to become more specialized." But she worries that, although CSR is now more strategic and sophisticated, it has shifted from something people were personally and directly passionate about, to, as she puts it, "a check in the box." I agree with her.

Milton Friedman may be rolling in his grave over the very notion of CSR as part and parcel of corporate structure and governance, but the professionalization of the discipline is not, in and of itself, a bad thing even for achieving the core business objectives he held sacred. It catalyzes repeatable practices. It puts good and meaningful topics on the agenda and invites accountability for achieving that agenda. It ensures a healthy pipeline of educated and ambitious talent. It creates opportunities for global acknowledgment, setting standards and raising the bar. The professionalization of CSR has done all this, and more.

Specialization, too, can be positive. It creates domains of expertise and promotes further research and understanding. It allows communities of shared interest to flourish and supports their further development. In the CSR space, specialization includes topics like sustainability, conflict zones, ethical sourcing, employee welfare, labor practices, health and safety, human rights, diversity, women's issues, government relations, and more. These are all vital areas of knowledge and practice, and they will form the pillars of the Conscience Economy.

But I sense that Jane misses the old days, when the mission for doing good while doing well was driven solely by passion, not professional ambition to get to the top of the CSR field and be the keynote speaker at one of the many CSR conferences that proliferate. It's tricky to critique something so well-intentioned. But I can't help but wonder: has it become a box to be checked, or worse, a perceived cost center that frustrates shareholders?

The Case Against CSR

A few weeks before I met with Jane, I had stopped by the library of the Cambridge Judge Business School to ask one of the librarians for her suggestions on books about CSR. She said, "And how about the anti-CSR movement?" I stopped in my tracks. It just seemed so...specific. An anti-CSR movement? But indeed, there are many who believe that CSR is worse than a check in a box. Companies use it as "greenwashing" to make it look like they're more ecologically balanced than they are. They use it as camouflage, or a cover-up, or for risk mitigation during tough crisis-management periods. I mention this to Jane. She's familiar with the concerns, of course. But she remains ardently in the pro-CSR camp. Or at least she's a fan of its highest intentions. "I'd just like to see it find its way into mainstream thinking."

My train is leaving in thirty minutes, and Jane has a meeting to get to, so I'm down to my last question for her. "What would you pitch today if you were back in a position of looking for corporate investment for social good?" Jane is quiet for a moment.

"I suppose the big question is, do you appeal to their self-interest or to their goodwill?" she says. "Because goodwill ultimately *is* self-interest." I smile. And then I sigh. So does Jane. Because she has landed on the gorgeous paradox that sits at the crux of the Conscience Economy. If only all business leaders saw it that way.

Fortunately, many leaders do, and this leads us to the next era, an era that came after Murphy's article was published, so I've gone ahead and named it myself. I believe that right now we're in the *performance era,* characterized by an ongoing quest to connect social impact with business performance. In the performance era, measurement is paramount. Proving that by making a positive impact companies also improve the bottom line is critical. The mantra of the performance era is "Do good *in order to* do well."

Concerns for employee welfare, which we saw earlier, continue but in new forms: diversity initiatives, scholarships, flextime, all sorts of new and customizable benefits for employees. Former Safeway CEO Steve Burd recently announced a program that incentivizes employees to take better care of their health, stating that, "Making money and doing good are not mutually exclusive."

In the performance era, a company's conscientiousness finds its way directly into the core message. Doing good is not just an additional activity designed to compensate for the necessary evil that ensues in the daily operations of enterprise.

The growing sense now is that by engaging in socially and environmentally impactful ways—for example, by producing products sustainably, employing a diverse workforce, or avoiding doing business with corrupt governments and thus supporting geopolitical conflicts—companies can have a positive effect on the bottom line. Social good is good for performance. It mitigates future risk. It builds trust that fuels cross-selling and up-selling and brand margin. It stabilizes predictability and forecasting. It motivates employee engagement and productivity. And it can even (as in the case of car-sharing subscription services like

Zipcar) drive innovation that leads not only to category disruption but even to triple-digit growth.

But things will not stop here. I've been peering into my virtual telescope, but to be truthful you don't have to look very far to see evidence of the next business prerogative to come. I call this next one the *initiative era,* when business is functioning within the precepts and cultural values of the Conscience Economy itself. In this era, business innovation begins with a mission of social impact that's as mission-critical to the enterprise as profit is today. And what was once called social responsibility or good corporate citizenship simply becomes good business.

It's time for CSR to stop being a specialized function and for its best intentions to suffuse the daily operations of business. It's time to embed CSR's skills and expertise into every function it can impact. Some questions for businesses to consider:

- Is your actual business model—not just its loftiest aspirations—driven by an expressed humane motive beyond profit? Could it be?
- If so, does leadership talk about it and reinforce it, regularly and consistently?
- Is your organization well-known for making a positive impact on society and the environment?
- Is such positive impact considered core to your value proposition, part of your operational procedures, or a philanthropic sideline?
- Are your performance incentives aligned with conscientious outcomes?
- Is your company's way of working making a quantifiably or qualitatively positive difference in the lives of people who *don't* work for you? Could it?
- Are the products or services you sell directly or indirectly empowering people to positively impact their lives, communities, the environment, and the world around them? Could they?

The Conscience Economy will be built by organizations that put positive social and environmental impact at the heart of business value creation. But without a specialized department, who's driving? Those tasked with leading the process should not only be its most vocal champions but those closest to your product, those closest to innovation and production, and those in closest relationship with your customers. That means the product and service innovators, designers, customer intimacy experts, creative storytellers, and communicators. And they will be led by a function that will resurrect and reinvigorate a function that is undergoing as creatively destructive a transformation as CSR: the marketing department.

6

The Death of Marketing

Marketing is under the microscope for good reason. It's about to die. At least, marketing as we've known it. This is not mere doomsday cynicism from engineering-focused skeptics or I-don't-trust-the-qualitative-stuff naysayers. "The future of marketing," the CEO of a prestigious London advertising agency openly confessed to me, "is for marketing to no longer exist." When I asked her why, she said matter-of-factly, "Because so much marketing is still just litter." The fact is, there's simply too much marketing competition, mostly delivered through one-way messaging. The average person is exposed to more than forty thousand messages a day. Litter indeed.

This CEO may well see her prediction come true, because there is perhaps no other function in the corporate array of specialties that's undergoing as much transformation and automation as marketing. Gone are the days when a chief marketing officer (whose tenure, though on the rise to forty-five months from a prior average of twenty-three, is still briefer than that of anyone else in the C-suite) can rise above the rank and file with a battery of Cannes Lions–winning advertising campaigns, creative retail promotions, and well-balanced spreadsheets of media spend.

Today, intelligent data analytics are a more effective way to reach profitable consumer prospects than a bold creative idea sprayed like artificial snow across the well-groomed slopes of the mediasphere. Creative ideas melt away under the hot lights of big data, while big data, as we know, is forever. A new arsenal of real-time and near-real-time metrics—including Net Promoter Scores, customer satisfaction data, and pipeline tracking, coupled with marketing and sales automation software—has changed the marketing function almost beyond recognition. It's no wonder some are calling for marketing to report to the chief information officer.

Data analytics, e-commerce, and social media have turned things upside down, as they typically do. The "channel mix" (as marketers refer to the array of modalities they use to deliver the business message) is more complicated and interwoven than ever before. Rest assured, as intelligent technologies continue to sweep through the enterprise, there's no function that's not going to have automation become a major efficiency driver. Marketing is today's playing field for transformation; it is on the front lines of change because it faces consumers and their transforming demands, and it can and should be at the heart of value creation.

Here's the dark secret about marketing today. No one is really sure what works. For every creative campaign that yields a measurable bump in sales, there's another that has zero impact. Even highly viral and buzzworthy marketing campaigns that correlate with rising sales figures are often bolstered with price reductions, which could be the real catalyst for volume pickup. There are so many levers, and new ones appear all the time (Twitter! Facebook! Vine!) with immediate claims of improved trackability and efficacy. Even the trademarked and near-sacred Net Promoter Score is under scrutiny as an effective success predictor by statisticians and management experts alike. And even new stalwarts like search engine optimization are frequently disrupted by updates to Google's algorithm.

Historically, the marketing department dreamt up ways to add value to a basic product, to make it easier for consumers to choose your product over your competitors'. Clever messages, jingles, and slogans were designed to distract potential buyers from whatever it is they were doing, to get their attention, and stick in their minds. It's fun to look at vintage images of major cities and see such an abundance of what, to our eyes today, read as beautifully naive product proclamations. Like the colorful din of shouting traders in the commodities futures pit at the Chicago Board of Trade, the marketplace was a cacophony of shouted announcements and blaring reinforcements—all communicated in one direction, of course—from the company to the consumer. By the early 1970s, as both product choice and leisure time grew, the marketplace became more competitive and more discerning. In response, marketing began focusing on identifying key messages and "big ideas" that would create a sense of memorable and emotional differentiation in the customer's mind. But even then, there were fewer consumers, fewer products, fewer channels, and consequently fewer choices and less clutter. Over the past decades, the cacophony has moved online. And it's gotten even more chaotic.

Going Online

I was literally in the room as part of the team that moved marketing from the physical world to the more pervasive digital world. Did you know that it was *Wired* magazine that planted the flag—or rather, the banner—of digital marketing on the web, where it has, to our surprise, remained fixed in place ever since? The place: early 1990s San Francisco (of course). Our South Park offices were far from glamorous, then. It was a dicey neighborhood. We were a true bootstrap start-up. There were bullet holes in the warehouse windowpanes. Occasionally, in the late hours, we'd hear a rat scuttle across the floorboards.

Louis Rossetto and Jane Metcalfe, the magazine's founders, had stated from the very first issue of the publication that their intent was not merely to create a magazine, but to build "a twenty-first-century media brand." The intent was to explore the media application of the emerging technologies that we covered in the print pages, and use these new technologies to experiment with the distribution of content. In effect, we were inverting the famous proclamation of the magazine's patron saint, Marshall McLuhan—for us, the message became the medium, and not vice versa.

And so it was that, as we came to understand the soon-coming possibilities of the web browser, Louis and Jane called a meeting to discuss how we might put some of our content on a web page. For some time, we'd been publishing articles on an AOL bulletin board. This new browser, Mosaic, would give us an opportunity to create something digital and desktop-accessible that looked more like the magazine and behaved more like commercial media.

But how would our online content be funded? After all, there would be costs associated with design and coding and hosting—just as there were costs associated with printing and distribution. What would the business model be? After all, no one had put commercial content on the web before. It was still the province of academia and government.

We decided to transport the tried-and-true media business model from the physical world to the virtual one: we would include advertising. The next question was, what form should this advertising take? A button? A distinct full or half or quarter page? Remember, the web was not yet a consumer channel. There were no interface or content design standards. It was unclear how we should even designate space. We knew that in order to convince an advertiser to pay for whatever space we gave them it would need to be highly visible, yet we didn't want to interrupt the content that the reader was really there to see. And so it was decided that a slim strip, like a piece of signage, could fit neatly on the top or the side of the page, like part of a frame. It wouldn't be too hard to code, it wouldn't be too distracting, but it would be visible enough that we could persuade an advertiser to try it.

The strip needed a name. Ad strip sounded naughty, but not in a good way. Then someone said "flag" and there was a buzz in the room. It sounded positive, but political. Someone else said, "What about banner, like a parade?" The strips did, we all agreed, look like banners. And the ad banner was born.

Unlike all advertising that preceded it, the banner was more than a message. It was the world's first dynamic link from media content to the advertiser. We delivered a customer directly to the advertiser for the first time—which meant that for the first time, advertisers had to figure out what to do with this new, more intimate and interactive dialogue. In one fell swoop, one-way advertising was over. The wall between business and customer was about to crumble.

None of us thought banners would last for two decades. We believed it was a temporary patch, and that far more sophisticated ways of marketing on the web would quickly supplant our cute and convenient banners. Looking back on that meeting, I must say, it was an extraordinary moment. We knew we were venturing into something historic. And two notable things happened immediately afterward. There were two resignations. One resigner left in fury to rejoin academia, stating (prophetically, I might add) that we'd just contaminated one of the last true frontiers for authentic human expression and connection with the most crass form of commercialism, advertising. The other resigner leased an office space in the same neighborhood, realizing (accurately) that we had just given birth to a multibillion-dollar industry, so he founded the world's first digital advertising agency.

Fast-forward to search engine optimization—which has replaced "the big idea" as the new holy grail. But just as we grew used to brainstorming SEO terms in our conference rooms, this contemporary discipline is being upended as Google updates its algorithms. It is emblematic that the iconic binoculars-shaped headquarters, designed by Frank Gehry in the early 1980s for then-iconic advertising agency Chiat/Day, are now inhabited by Google, as a Venice Beach-side extension of the Googleplex. The cafés of Venice Beach, California, have long been frequented by the kind of young, casual, confident people who know they're working in a glamour industry. Today, the glamour industry is search technology, the infrastructure that holds all communication—and seemingly, our lives—together.

This puts a big fat question mark next to the old trope of creative big ideas as communication drivers. Can I tell you how many marketing executives of a certain age still talk glowingly about Apple's big idea of "Think Different," and use it as an example of iconic marketing even today? Yet it's well over a decade out of date. Most people were still using fax machines when that campaign ran in 1997. It's time to lovingly consign it to the history museum. I find it a classic example of change resistance that big ideas, at least as we used to think of them, remain the highest aspiration of most blue-chip advertising agencies and many of their clients. Because it bears noting that Apple itself doesn't deploy big ideas in their marketing anymore. They put them where they belong—at the heart of their product strategy.

Whatever your beliefs about mortality, there is life after death for The Employees Formerly Known As Marketers. Because healthy, profitable business relationships and breakthrough value creation and delivery in the Conscience Economy will require a set of lateral skills and aptitudes. Right and left brain, working in alignment. Meaning making, story telling, communicating in a relevant way with different functions, creativity, competitive foresight, human insight, relationship management, social interaction, organizational psychology—these are the kinds of talents that every future-proof business will require at the crux of value creation.

Many, if not most, of these skills sit underutilized and marginalized in marketing departments today. Decades ago, management guru Peter Drucker made an observation that was years ahead of its time: "Because the purpose of business is to create a customer, the business enterprise has two—and only two—basic functions: marketing and innovation. Marketing and innovation produce results; all the rest are costs. Marketing is the distinguishing, unique function of the business."

Not marketing as we've known it, though, with its outbound-communications mandate. It's time to banish that to the proverbial dustheap of history. Meet its successor: the role that is chiefly responsible for the nexus of value creation in the Conscience Economy enterprise. Meet your new CMO: chief *matchmaking* officer.

The Matchmaking Mandate

The mandate of your chief matchmaking officer and her team is fourfold.

1. To identify those people most likely to connect with your brand, buy its products or services, work for you, advocate for you, create value for you, innovate with you, and help your business grow. In other words, the mandate is not just to identify your market, but the entire holistic ecosystem of human relationships that create business value.

2. To learn and understand *everything* about these people—how they think and feel about the world as well as about your business, what they value, their deepest hopes and highest aspirations, their spending power, their social influence, where they are, how their needs and feelings and behaviors change depending upon where they are—and the best, most personal, least creepy and invasive way to connect with them.

3. To apply those learnings about needs, desires, and demands, both latent and explicit, to every relevant operation in the company. This includes everything from corporate strategy to product innovation and positioning to government policy to communications, but especially to business innovation. The goal is ensuring that human, social, and environmental requirements become the guiding specifications for the

next round of products, services, and operating procedure—which are, in the Conscience Economy, part of the business product itself.

4. To establish and sustain the connection—to make a successful and lasting match—between people and your business, creating long-term, trusting relationships that drive value and profit into the enterprise while generating positive impact in the wider world.

Straightforward stuff, right?

For a matchmaker, it's all in a day's work. Because unlike most other corporate functions, matchmakers understand and deal in two often opposing strains of information that drive business success—the rational facts and the emotional truths. Matchmakers are that rare combination of right-brained *and* left-brained. They can interpret data without being in its thrall. They can confidently apply creative intuition and emotional intelligence to translate a range of factual and measurable inputs into meaningful and actionable insight. They understand the transformative power of storytelling, and they are masters of behavior-changing communication. They are a personified mash-up of the creative communication skills embodied in marketers of yore and the future-friendly analytical skills of information-obsessed digital natives.

In the Conscience Economy, matchmaking is never, ever considered a cost center. And it's definitely not an internal service provider that's brought in at the end of the value-creation cycle. The things that matter most to citizens of the Conscience Economy—the things they are willing to spend the most on—are meaningful, emotional, and enlightened. Which is not to say that the Conscience Economy isn't driven by pragmatism. Zoom out—way, way out—and we can see that the drive for collective self-actualization is sensible indeed in order to preserve a healthy and thriving society, but it's also the apex of emotional intelligence. The matchmaker ensures that this emerging and growing human need is satisfied and that it is, for the business, profitable.

So what about the traditional four Ps of marketing: product, positioning, promotion, and pricing? Dead and buried? Hardly. They will undergo a shape-shift and a re-sort.

The Five Cs of Matchmaking

As capabilities and customer expectations of convenience, engagement, and meaningfulness have advanced, the matchmaker has a new set of considerations and competencies to apply. Exit the Ps, enter the Cs. Five of them: context, conversation, clarity, cohesion, and creativity.

Context

In the Conscience Economy, people have a firm grasp (literally—it's in their hands) of the potential contextual capabilities of technology, and, consequently, expect personalization and convenience. Yet the daily utility of contextual technology is still in its embryonic stage.

Marketers—and particularly those with a media-planning bent—used to create (and I suspect many still do) what we called a touchpoint plan. I've personally sat through endless revisions of such plans, which typically presumed a rather predictable and linear "consumer journey." This journey proceeded through a narrative cycle of phases borrowed from the sales funnel, for example "awareness," "consideration," "product trial," "purchase," "out-of-the-box first use," and "advocacy." These phases would include moments like waiting at a bus stop, watching TV, or driving past a billboard. At particular "touchpoints," the marketer would drop in a piece of strategic marketing, like Hansel and Gretel's breadcrumbs, creating a pathway of clever, synchronized, gradually building messages, all the way to the point of sale, where there would be ever more hard-driving sales messages and a particular selling experience. All very logical. Except that it isn't anymore. And hasn't been for a while.

It's a cheap shot to even mention that no living person you or I know has ever ventured out on a "consumer journey." But if he did, it would start and end in two places only: online or in a store. We research the products we buy, extensively. And if we don't buy them then and there, online, we go to a store to sample, try on, try out, browse, touch, taste, and even, sometimes, to socialize with other people who are doing the same thing. Everything else is interruption, disruption, and in the background.

Now seems like a good time to mention that, having spent many years as a marketer, I happen to be a fan of outdoor and transit advertising.

When it's done right, it can actually add design, beauty, and wit to the built environment. It can also measurably increase awareness of your offering—but only when it's designed simply to do that. There aren't many companies willing to invest a significant outdoor media budget to provide a mere flash of information, and even a bit of brightness and charm to enhance the everyday. Use it for more than that, though, and you've gone from smart to creating marketing litter.

But, oh, the number of times I've sat in meetings where the mock-ups for every poster, every billboard, every online banner—every piece of communication—were debated ad infinitum because of the company's desire to load up on all kinds of information about as many product features as we could cram legibly into the layout. Those rich and informative product messages belong online and at the point of sale, and absolutely *nowhere* else.

Because context is everything. And when you're waiting for the bus or driving down the highway, if you even happen to be thinking about buying something, you are not searching billboards to find it. You might, on the other hand, be searching on your mobile device. It's remarkable how this basic logic (a reasonably bright third grader could grasp it) escapes even seasoned executives.

The matchmaker understands far more than a mere media lay-down. She understands the multiple layers and conditions that comprise a person's context. Because context is not only geospatial, it's temporal, emotional, and circumstantial. It's not only *where* you are, it's *how* you are. It's emotional and circumstantial. It includes the time of year, the time of day or night. Are you hungry? Is it hot out? Are you with friends? Are you in your car? Where are you going, and why? Every context yields a need to state that your business may have a better way of satisfying.

Here's the tricky part, and the reason that there is a delicate and sophisticated art to matchmaking in context: there is nothing more spooky or more of an immediate turnoff than a company message that gets delivered in such a way that it demonstrates we're being watched.

A contextual strategy starts with understanding the most likely conditions for influencing a sale. But it goes broader and deeper than "you need it now so buy it now." The matchmaker leverages contexts for consumer advocacy and promotion. Contexts for up-selling or cross-selling. Contexts for educating someone on how to best use your offering. The next generation of media strategy will be contextual strategy, which will seek to match you, the consumer, with the very thing you want and need at that moment, at a good price.

The matchmaker creates new kinds of real-time promotions based upon fluctuating demand and location. A bit of artificial intelligence that analyzes real-time behavior and contextual conditions (the day, the time, the temperature, etc.) will make it increasingly possible to connect in-the-moment needs with exactly the right offering. Even pricing is contextual. A new umbrella is worth more the moment it starts to rain. But matchmaker beware: conditional and contextual pricing can be hazardous to your brand if it manifests as exploitative and greedy, as ridesharing service Uber learned when it experienced a full-on social media backlash because it raised prices for rides on rainy Friday nights, resulting in fares upward of $200 for routes that would regularly cost far less.

Conversation

I'm jetlagged in Beijing, downing my third black coffee in an enormous conference room on the top floor of the company's Chinese head office. My colleagues and I have flown in from European headquarters, not only to break bread with the local marketing team but to share with them the newest iteration of company strategy. The renewed strategy, designed to inform product innovation as well as marketing and sales, is driven by fresh insights about an underserved but deep and globally distributed human motivation—the desire to live a more adventurous life.

Because this desire for adventure is a new type of need, one that the company is utterly unused to meeting, the strategy is, shall we say, controversial. Indeed, there are pockets of skepticism across the company about our findings, and resistance abounds. So we've not only arrived to talk in person; we've brought in a bunch of external people, potential customers—some of whom are loyal to our products, but most of whom aren't—to share their own everyday life stories with us. In Mandarin, of course, so I sit close to the translator. She's almost breathless as she tries to keep pace with the enthusiastic conversation that's happening in front of us.

I must admit, when the group of customers enters the room, my heart sinks a little. They simply don't look like people who are going to get fired up about living adventurously. They are neither fashion-forward nor athletic. They aren't flashing bold, charismatic smiles or standing tall with entrepreneurial conviction. They're regular Beijingers. But then they start to answer questions from my local colleagues. And the room catches fire.

"I really want to turn my life upside down and travel the world," says a meek-looking young woman in a pale pink sweater. "I like to do things differently than anyone has ever done them before," says the slightly pudgy guy in wire-rimmed glasses. "Every weekend I can get away, I choose a different mountain to climb," says a neatly dressed, professional-looking woman, "and sometimes I get my husband to come too." "I'm teaching myself to cook Italian food because I like learning new things," says another customer. And then the money shot, from what looks like the youngest person in the group: "I want my life to be an adventure every day." This, in China, a civilization with centuries of non-individualistic, pro-communal bias. But also a society where the world is changing so fast that life indeed is an adventure every day.

It's not that the insights themselves are so profound—indeed, this is exactly why we'd built the strategy we are there to advocate. But the conversation changes everything—it shatters walls of resistance and opens up possibilities for reinvention.

Business is built on relationships, and relationships are built, strengthened, and sustained through dialogue. This has never been more true than it is now, with social media channels and real-time conversation still growing. Customers expect a high degree of interactivity and engagement—on their own terms. Matchmaking happens best when the right conversation facilitates a closer connection.

Your business and brand are part of an ongoing dialogue, and the matchmaker's job is to ensure open participation, to create conditions and circumstances for interactive communication. Not only online, but everywhere, including product demonstration experiences and events. The matchmaker will consider how the merchandising environment itself becomes a more conversational space, where sales staff can converse with customers and where consumers can socialize with one another.

It's about more than using the conversation to sell. It's about harvesting insights from the interaction to discover and recommend new product features. The conversation itself is useful and value generating, but the insights from the dialogue have a second life, deeper in your business, as they drive the optimization of new sources of value, whether it's a more efficient delivery system, a new product feature, a line extension, a potential retail location, or a more effective promotional message. There's little need for old-school market research when the matchmaker is in near constant dialogue, channeling a continuous stream of customers' opinions, desires, and needs into the organization. Matchmakers are tasked with building and maintaining a communications system—both digital and interpersonal—that ensures that real-time insight makes its way to those corners of the enterprise where it can be swiftly converted into value.

If this sounds too jargony, I'll try it in plain English. The moment a matchmaker (or his software) catches a pattern of conversation that suggests people are frustrated with wait times for customer service, that input goes immediately to the customer service department, not into a report. The moment a matchmaker sees people getting worked up about an impending bill that's on the legislative agenda, it gets channeled to communications, where the company's point of view in light of said bill gets immediately channeled back out to the public. It's about removing latency, staying current, and constantly positioning the organization at the forefront of what is most important to the people it serves.

The matchmaker is both the host and the catalyst of these conversations. And the conversations are not only about products and brands. In the Conscience Economy, the matchmaker engages people in those issues most on their minds. The matchmaker jumps in on those conversations that are already flourishing across society, but also builds programs that provide a reason for conversation about an issue, an aspiration, a dream, or an urgent development for which your business happens to have a solution.

A blend of social technology and intelligent analytics will play a huge role in managing, synchronizing, and harvesting applicable insights from myriad simultaneous interactions. But not every conversation has to be technologically enabled. Personal, physical interactions are the most powerful conversations of all, and the matchmaker will regularly introduce people—in person—from various functions to the real-life customers your business serves. As we saw in Beijing, there's nothing quite like getting to know someone in person for changing your point of view.

Your goal is not only to be a company people talk about. Your goal is to learn from what you hear and apply it, so that you're a company people love.

Clarity

With so much more to monitor, clarity is more important than ever before. Because the Conscience Economy places value not only on what your product does, but on how you produce it, the impact your operations have on the world, how you treat your people, your political biases, and more, there's never been more to communicate. But we can only handle so much—our lives are overloaded with information as it is. So the matchmaker must distill a broad range of facts into an initiative, a brief, a recommendation, or a report that is not only meaningful but actionable.

In an era of exponentially proliferating data and analytics, the matchmaker is a sense maker. The matchmaker filters, streamlines, and interprets insights and foresights for the rest of the organization. Matchmaking is not just monitoring data and content, but making the inherent revelations of that data clear and applicable.

Clarity includes transparency, that chic term that the Global Language Monitor—a service that does exactly what its title says, it monitors language globally—puts way up on its current business buzzword list. The matchmaker is responsible for ensuring that truth is shared in all directions, for ensuring that authentic information cuts through the clutter. It's vital to identify those things that are going to be particularly meaningful to each stakeholder. In the Conscience Economy, this includes sharing how the business works, the impact of its operations, and suggestions for using its products to better the world. This content will not only be sourced from within, but from the community of customers, suppliers, producers, and fans who are engaged with your business.

Real-time digital capability enables matchmakers to experiment with a range of different messages to assess, adapt, and deploy those that are most effective. This doesn't negate the importance of powerful communication and great writing; in the Conscience Economy, the more emotionally astute your message, the more powerful it will be. But we now have a means of getting better feedback sooner, to make the adjustments necessary to drive not only a successful sale but effective outcomes across the enterprise. In other words, the matchmaker potentially holds the key to the continuous improvement of all business functions, from HR to operations. Driving sales is foremost, but every aspect of organizational life will benefit from real-time feedback and clear communication.

If information is the lifeblood of contemporary enterprise, great matchmaking will be the heart and circulatory system of business, pumping useful, clear, truthful information into every muscle of the body, strengthening it and enabling it to move forward and grow.

Cohesion

Cohesion means getting things (and people) to stick together and work together. The matchmaker builds and sustains mutually advantageous, profitable connections between the business and its customers. By analyzing data, while leveraging intuitive insight and foresight, she discovers patterns and opportunities in the continuous conversations she manages and facilitates. She identifies those people who are most likely to buy from you, to promote you, to best represent you—and develops the means to engage them, close the sale, and help them connect with others on your (and their) behalf. At any given moment, people need or desire something, and the matchmaker has the intelligence and the empathy to know exactly when to provide the right product at the right time.

Cohesion is also about maintaining communications and brand consistency, so that you're recognized and attractive no matter where a customer is. A matchmaker establishes, and when necessary rigorously enforces, the protocols that ensure everyone is executing plans in concert. This includes the alignment of globally developed and business-critical identity and strategy with local cultural nuances and local sales needs. This is the classic dilemma of international marketing: the right balance between global and local control.

The Conscience Economy is more decentralized than any that precedes it, and thus the notion of "control" is in many ways outdated. This is why cohesion is a more useful aspiration than control. Local markets and global headquarters are not in opposition; and it will become increasingly easy for them to be in constant conversation. The matchmaker ensures that frontline input is truly at the core of everything emanating from the head office. Meanwhile, local matchmakers must acknowledge and embrace the idea that, for the local customer, a significant amount of the perceived value of a global offering is in the fact that it is global; therefore, alignment with international standards is vital. Local consumers who choose global brands are making a choice to be part of something international, to be part of something bigger.

There is no such thing as the "right" amount of local adaptation. It's a question of economic efficiency. Utilizing international assets rather than re-producing over and over again is obviously more cost effective than broadly distributed origination, and in an increasingly globally astute world, customers can see your brand from multiple international angles. Fragmentation doesn't build confidence; coherence does.

Indeed, as long as consistency standards are kept, brand behaviors are adhered to, and a program is recognizably the voice of one company, locally generated programs can be the most effective of all.

Perhaps the most important aspects on which your matchmaker can ensure coherence are social and environmental impact, the causes and issues that people care about, and your product offering. By driving innovation and generating a coherent set of product specifications that emerge from the matchmaking process, the matchmaker can ensure cohesion between your brand and everything you do and sell.

Creativity

There are whole tomes on the science and the art of creativity. I will ruthlessly hyper-summarize from them: unlike most other quantitative business processes, creativity can neither be automated nor rigorously engineered. Creativity can only thrive in a context where ideas can flow, prototypes can be made, inspiration is abundant, and risky ideas can be explored without consequence. Creative talent requires a very different leadership and management style than nearly every other function in the enterprise. And creativity needs a different type of physical environment as well. A creative studio is as different from an office as a park is from a factory. This is why so many companies outsource their creative processes and creative output to agencies and design firms. Outsourcing ensures that the process is, in effect, protected from the exigencies of daily business.

This is a shame, because creativity and its offspring—innovation—are your primary sources of business value. Outsourcing creative execution makes sense, but outsourcing value creation itself makes no sense. In the Conscience Economy, the product *is* the message. And thus, the matchmaker is responsible for creating a safe and inspiring environment within the enterprise that enables creative idea generation and innovation to flourish, from physical space and creative tools to a stream of stimulus for new ideas.

The matchmaker also works closely with your financial team to generate rich, meaningful, and actionable integrated reporting, connecting the right people and functions inside and outside the organization with the right information from both inside and outside the organization. Because the matchmaker is as fluent in analytics as she is skilled at storytelling, she is able to lead the translation of data into meaning.

In the Conscience Economy, the rich overlap between product features, production processes, and social impact is the source of differentiating sales messages, and thus, the matchmaker holds ultimate responsibility for product innovation and design. Because she is driving the conversation with customers, she can feed learnings directly into value creation—product innovation, design, user interface, sales messages, and more. The matchmaker translates business intelligence and real-time customer insight into a clear definition of product and sales messaging requirements. Great matchmakers are organizations' ultimate champions of innovation. The ultimate goal: to create new ways of meeting social and environmental challenges and embedding them in the brand offering. Positive impact is the primary guiding principle for creativity.

Innovation is increasingly a collaborative and collective process. The matchmaker's most powerful approach to innovating business value will be to facilitate the sharing of true stories and rich experiences—about your products as well as your business processes themselves—that move people and bring them together for common cause. By creating meaningful reasons to buy, matchmakers will increase customer desire for your products and services, as well as the improvement of our world.

7

Collective Innovation

Creativity is humanity's greatest power, yet in business we usually marginalize it. No other species beyond *Homo sapiens* is fundamentally creative for the sake of it. Animals may build nests, camouflage themselves, or make sounds that seem like music, but when they do, it's for utility alone, not an act of creativity. Animals don't make art or music for pleasure. Creativity is in no small part what makes us human.

We are also social beings. We need one another in order to thrive. We are literally better together. Not just happier, but more effective and more conscientious. Combine our social nature with our creative nature, and together we are a powerhouse for human progress. Breakthrough innovation has become a collective process.

This is in no small part attributable to our increasingly collective sense of identity. The dialectic between "I" and "we" is shifting. On one hand, the proliferation of "selfies" across the web would suggest a tendency to use media as a mirror. Self-empowerment and a more selfish orientation might seem to be the future. But a closer look reveals a different truth: me *is* we, for a new generation of people. Years of assumed and ubiquitous connectedness have eroded the boundary between self and other, creating new forms of tribalism that are no longer dependent upon geographic proximity. A scan of social media sites, and particularly individual comments and posts, shows the extent to which people feel and express deeply personal outrage about issues that are far from their own physical reality. Ubuntu, the African notion of a collective identity I described earlier, is becoming a natural state of consciousness for increasing numbers of people.

Smartphones and tablets enable us to cognitively inhabit multiple places and contexts at once. We can communicate in real time with others who aren't physically with us even as we sit in the presence of people who are. We can have meta-conversations in the on-screen chat window while we're having a physical meeting in the conference room (an addictive habit among execs at one company I worked with, and a strategic approach to conference calls at another). Digital context, which used to be confined to the desktop, is now mobile. We can be online chatting and in the mall shopping (or vice versa) at the same time. I call this phenomenon "concurrency." Our physical and digital contexts can be merged, or kept separate, concurrently.

This concurrency didn't exist even ten years ago. One could say that the impact is a shorter attention span. And who hasn't felt abandoned when the person across the table is more engaged in the virtual than the physical experience? I'm certainly guilty of the instant opt-out-by-checking-WhatsApp. Many have tried to establish universal principles of smartphone etiquette, so far to no avail. I think time will tell. (We used to smoke in the office, too.) Bad manners aside, this multipresence capability has pluses that outweigh the minuses. We will grow more fluent in it as it becomes part of regular life and not just a new addiction to in-the-moment escapism. We'll develop a more nuanced sense of identity and relationship to others. We will literally feel a sense of closeness that doesn't require physical presence. Not only with friends, but with strangers and their circumstances far from our home. It's already happening. People join forces virtually to elect leaders, express joy or outrage about current issues, support causes, and create software together.

Thanks to its intrepid pioneer origins, the United States is a paragon of the individualistic mind-set, a way of thinking that's quite different from the communal orientation of Eastern cultures. Individual independence and freedom are paramount, and not just among the gun lobbyists. Yet young people in general are beginning to look more similar around the world. Cultures that traditionally held a collective sensibility at their core, like China and India, are beginning to seem less alien. I was amazed by a video, produced by a consumer insight team at MTV and shown to me by the head of marketing at Viacom. It depicted, documentary-style, what the team had learned about the next generation of citizens in the United States. The young people in the video represented a spectrum of backgrounds and cultural predilections. As you'd expect, they talked about their passions and hobbies, from skateboarding to cake baking to sports and more. But their most moving and shared attribute: they all valued their parents, wider family, friends, and community over all else. Despite the cliches about self-centered youth, market research suggests that this new cohort is the most family focused, most socially empathetic generation that's ever been studied.

Because they've never experienced life without being connected to one another, they're used to continuous sharing and communication. They're fluent in multiple modalities of simultaneous communication, from Snapchat and Instagram to WhatsApp to Skype. And they are also fluent in making their own media, contributing their points of view, and commenting on virtually everything they encounter online. They have never known media that wasn't manipulatable, hackable, re-editable, and socially shareable. They have never known a world in which they couldn't broadcast their opinion. They can build audiences for their ideas in the tens of thousands. Creativity has never been more democratic than it is today.

The merging of these tendencies—toward a collective sense of identity, a motivation to constantly express and share, and a deepening sense of connection to family and community—is a powerful creative catalyst; indeed, it's a hallmark of the Conscience Economy. If connectivity is the cause of the emerging Conscience Economy, collective innovation is its engine.

There are two modes of working together toward an outcome. There's consensus building, which focuses on getting a usually broadly diverse group with different priorities to be aligned and moving in the same direction. And there's true collaboration, which is getting a group of people, and sometimes even a massive group, to work together to create something new. One is an unparalleled force for engagement in change. The other is an innovation killer.

Consensus: The Innovation Killer

There's a chasm of difference between consensus and collaboration. When it comes to the Conscience Economy, not understanding those differences can be fatal, if not for people than for ideas.

Consensus is a viable and even admirable aspiration in certain contexts, for example, democratic governance and development of actionable policies in the public sphere. But in the workplace, it's an innovation murderer. Whereas true collaboration can be the most potent innovation catalyst there is.

Consensus and collaboration can look deceptively similar, and in some cases, the terms are even used interchangeably. Be vigilant here, because the word "collaboration" is far too often used to mean consensus. That's because most big organizations really, really like consensus. They don't like rocking the boat. They like when everyone gets along, when everyone agrees. Indeed, the whole business culture of the Nordic countries is famously consensus driven. If the group can't buy into a decision unanimously, the idea won't go forward.

But of course, everyone can't agree. That's the beauty of our human diversity, our wide range of experiences, our genetic complexity. Agreeing is not always good. After all, it's disagreement that fuels progress. When we have the grace to disagree but trust that another way could generate new options, we open up the possibility of remaking the world around us. When we stick with our own opinions, or focus our energy on trying to get others onto our page, we often miss out on the benefits of creative abrasion.

Of course, building consensus is a skill that is frequently listed in executive headhunter briefs for high-level job specs. Indeed, most boards of directors and leadership teams make decisions by consensus, in one way or another.

Meanwhile, "empowering collaboration" is a term used less frequently. Strange, when you think about it. Because collaboration is by far the more powerful approach, and when you do it right, there's no need to build consensus later. The solution is so robust, because it's been built by those who have a vested interest in its success, that choosing to execute is simply logical. Engaging people in the process doesn't just win them over, it ensures that the solution is their own.

Here's why consensus building can be so dangerous to innovation. Innovating is about introducing something new, something that hasn't been seen before. Consensus is about agreement and usually involves a measure of compromise.

Innovation is about leaning into what's uncomfortable, exploring new possibilities, and venturing outside the security and relief of the known. When building consensus, the tendency of those included is to take stuff out, to break stuff down, and to look for areas that are uncomfortable, address them, and, ideally, to sand them down. Consensus smooths the edges, like the action of waves on a stone. It's a reductive process.

But innovation needs sharp and jagged edges. It's about creating something different, surprising, risky, and therefore often initially unpopular. Collaboration is, at its best, an additive process. It's great for innovation. Because when you put unlikely ingredients together, instead of taking them out, you get something new. It's catalytic to transformation, instead of a hindrance.

I've been experimenting with collective innovation for nearly two decades. Three particular cases stand out as useful models for application across a range of business challenges. One is a hyperlocal community cocreation project, one is a globally crowdsourced social and digital creative project, and the third is a rapid prototyping process.

Community Cocreation

Projects that sit at the confluence of complicated community debates—particularly in the public sector—require a delicate balance of diplomatic acumen, empathy, and forthrightness. They can languish or flourish, depending upon the motivation of all involved.

As recently as a decade ago, San Francisco's Castro District, an area that's perhaps the world's most famous district of gay men and women, had no local men's health center. Considering the range of public health issues—from drug abuse to mental health to runaways to sexually transmitted infections—impacting the community, as well as its political activism and strong sense of inclusive identity, this lack of a neighborhood health hub was both surprising and odd.

But then something equally surprising and odd happened. A pot of funding appeared, dedicated to creating just such a facility, right smack in the geographic heart of the area. It was miraculous, but utterly loaded with, shall we say, *issues*. For one thing, some said it was blood money.

In fact, it was a settlement payout from one of the big pharma companies. The San Francisco AIDS Foundation, one of the oldest and most prestigious organizations in the fight against HIV/AIDS, had taken issue with the fact that HIV medications were being marketed with what the foundation claimed was misleading, overly aspirational imagery. Uplifting photographs of hale and hearty, muscular young men climbing mountains, the argument went, gave people the impression that contracting HIV was no problem, and that with proper treatment, it might even lead a person to be more healthy and attractive than before. Such advertising, went the argument, might persuade people to be less concerned about risky behaviors, and thus expand the market for—and dependence on—particular medications.

A group of community activists, in partnership with the foundation, made some noise about it, and in recompense the corporation in question provided some funding, earmarked for the creation of a facility in the Castro that would address the community's unique needs.

Now, imagine. It's San Francisco, a place as consistently progressively vocal every day of the week as a boisterous march on Washington. The city is peopled by a bunch of intensely motivated, highly educated community activists, many of them themselves living with a treatable but ever life-threatening disease. And suddenly a pot of money appears. Who was going to decide how it would be spent? What would it be spent on? How would the conversation even be conducted?

Some months before, I had expressed some interest in local politics to a colleague and acquaintance of mine who was also a consultant at the Bridgespan Group, a nonprofit offshoot of Bain & Company that focuses on providing blue-chip-quality strategic management advice to community and nonprofit organizations. In addition to his day job, Don was deeply involved in local community work. As I spoke the words, "I've thought about learning more about public office," he gave me a wry smile and said, "You have no idea how complicated it can be. Corporations are a picnic compared to community." Anyway, when The Money appeared, he invited me to join the group that had self-organized in order to establish how to spend it. I wonder if his agenda was to permanently dissuade me from my local government aspirations, but what he actually said was that he thought I might be able to help.

One conversation led to another, but it was increasingly clear to me that we would never reach consensus. No one was going to agree on anything. We couldn't even agree on whether it was okay to suggest that HIV itself was a bad thing.

But we had a crisis on our hands, and an opportunity to do something about it. We had to find a way to move forward and innovate together, fast.

So together, we created a process that I now refer to as social design. One of the best things about working with the group was how open they were to inventing new ways of doing things. And I think it's this very openness to transformation that led to what happened next.

Rather than come up with a design for the facility ourselves, we decided to invite and commission the community itself to design it. Not to comment on a preestablished program and not to just check the boxes of community approval, but to actually design the place itself.

We had a unique situation in that we knew the property we were going to rent. We had a location. We just didn't know what to do with it. So we began, as so many things do, on the street. We "pre-branded" ourselves The Castroguys, so we wouldn't just be strangers on the street, we'd be a friendly group of concerned and interested citizens. We designed tee shirts, whipped up an identity, and out we went with our clipboards (tablets had yet to be invented) to ask people on the street what they'd like to see in the neighborhood. At the end of our conversations, we asked if they'd be interested in joining the community design team. After hundreds of interviews, we recruited about thirty people from the neighborhood to come be part of the next step in the process.

We ran a series of workshops with these people—and paid them to be there. We provided only the most basic briefing of requirements—that the facility was going to be a community center with a focus on health. But it didn't have to be a clinic. It could be anything that the group designed.

First, each breakout group created personas that represented the type of person who would use the place. They had to make up a realistic character, name him or her, and describe the character in sufficient detail so that they could then model an experience that the persona would most appreciate.

Then we provided a blueprint of the raw space, and asked people to imagine what sorts of things could happen inside. What would they see? Who would they meet? Who would help them? How would they move through the space? What sorts of things would happen there? Most importantly, what sorts of things would attract them to come the first time, and what would cause them to return?

As the various groups worked through their scenarios, some design principles emerged organically from their collaboration. For example, most people thought their persona would feel uncomfortable being seen going into a place that was explicitly health oriented. They attached stigma to the need to visit clinical services, and the very visibility of the location right in the middle of a main shopping and entertainment district eliminated any possibility of discretion. So the facility needed to have an overt purpose above and beyond health services. It needed to function as a community center, a hive of social activity. Even if a client was going to the place for a diagnosis, it would also be possible that he was attending an art opening or shopping for neighborhood-themed gifts.

Another emergent requirement from the groups was the idea that the physical space itself be laid out and "zoned" to address a number of different kinds of interaction (or non-interaction) with other people, from "leave me alone" anonymity to a full-on consultation with a staff member. I dubbed this emergent and surprising spatial segmentation "zones of intimacy."

Our steering committee's initial assumption, prior to the social design workshops, was that it would be good to have a greeter or a concierge right by the door, to welcome people as they entered. But once the groups got their hands on the design process, it became obvious that this could be a turnoff. Health issues can be sensitive, and a buoyant "Hello!" is not necessarily the appropriate response if someone is coming in with a problem, especially if the problem is connected to mental health. Groups designed an experience that put the greeter at the *back* of the space. The further in you enter, the more "intimate" the interaction can be. Visitors could explore the space at their own pace. When they first walk in, they'd be in an "anonymous" zone—not greeted, able to land at their particular comfort level. If they had further questions, they could approach the concierge in the back.

These interaction protocols and spatial allocation principles—all designed by the community who would be clients of the program—became vital when ultimately specifying how the facility would both be laid out and actually operate. And these solutions and uses of space never would have occurred to clinicians, architects, health professionals, or even retail designers. Or, for that matter, me. Collective innovation yielded a breakthrough solution that turned out to be robust as well.

As a result, Magnet was born, and ten years on, it proudly continues to surpass its own service goals. It's a testament to the power of collaborative innovation and the efficacy of inviting the people a product or service is meant to benefit to help in its design. Looking back, I realize that a full five years before the term was even coined, we were crowdsourcing.

Creative Crowdsourcing

Arguably, it all started with the open source software movement, which had its genesis in collaborative software development in the '60s and reached critical mass around the turn of the millennium. The principle of openly publishing source code so that others can use it, modify it, and improve it is aligned with the values of the Conscience Economy. Collective innovation can generate extensive and valuable assets. In effect, systems and solutions built on open source platforms can offer more value because they are inherently interrelated and thus are more likely to be compatible and extensible—and thus more useful.

There are suggestions that mere open source is not conscientious enough—that the information needed to make it easy to manipulate and add to a programming system should be embedded in the release itself. The movement is on a trajectory toward radical openness, proactively including the actual tools and means for breaking into and remaking not only software, but in time, nearly anything at all.

Crowdsourcing, a term coined in 2006, is becoming a viable approach to innovation. Whether you invite social participation in the development of a solution or not, the new generation's natural tendency will be to want to get involved. What's interesting about crowdsourcing as a philosophy and a technique is that it breaks down previous notions of individual expertise. It is also a means of engaging an intended customer or audience in your offering.

My marketing team and I once developed an international advertising campaign entirely from crowdsourced imagery. The campaign was all about noticing the amazing, strange, and beautiful things that can happen in everyday life and sharing them through pictures. We believed that by collecting spontaneous images taken by amateur photographers and ordinary people (though is anyone really ordinary?) who were simply documenting in their everyday, unscripted lives, by collecting *their* everyday amazing experiences, we'd generate a conversation. The solicitation itself was a communication opportunity, while the outcome would be an ever-growing catalog of images that were an authentic reflection of our target consumer.

It wasn't easy to do. In fact, I had to do significant persuading to convince everyone both on my team and at our agency that it would be worth it to *not* simply call a photographer and commission imagery. As my creative partners at the agency pointed out (and subsequently brilliantly executed), we had to create a whole new process along with incentives to motivate people to submit their photos. We had to offer guidelines for what we wanted and why without being so prescriptive that we'd shut down creativity. We had to build a new web-based infrastructure and content management system for the solicitation, collection and sorting, and editing and selection of images. We had to put a payment system in place, figure out rights management, and more. Although in the end it was only marginally less expensive than hiring a photographer, it was definitely a lot more work to get it up and running. That's the key here: changing the process adds work. At first. It will not happen automatically. Do I even need to say that consensus would have killed the idea?

It was an experiment. And the results were rewarding. Not only did we collect some wonderfully evocative images of circumstances we never would have imagined ourselves, we also had the happy accident of seeing themes emerge. The images submitted were representations of moments in our customers' lives that were, to them, everyday but significant. A bonus: in the process, we received near-real-time, visual market insight.

Thanks to the exponential increase of digital and mobile photography, our visual acuity is growing. People can immediately tell the difference between a professionally generated image (the company is trying to sell me something) and a peer-generated image (the company is including me in a conversation). With crowdsourcing, both the process and the outcome generate value for both sides. It can be a win–win.

Rapid Prototyping

When it comes to collective innovation, faster is better. Rapid prototyping is an energizing and effective technique for harnessing the power of collective innovation.

Here's why fast could be the new slow. Like the risk aversion that plagues consensus, our own minds have a tendency to avoid risk. And so as we are imagining things, a little voice will edit the idea before it has a chance to take its first tiny breath. Logic is strong and ingrained. It's a survival strategy. But our imaginations can outrun our logic, if we commit to creating quickly.

The "prototyping" part of the term is about making—not just discussing. I'm the last person who's going to put discussion on the naughty step, but there are times (and collaboration, ironically, can be one of them) when discussion, however well-intentioned, shuts down possibility rather than opening it up.

At a regional creativity conference recently, I led a group of young professionals—nearly all under thirty-five years old—from across Europe to practice the rapid prototyping technique, but with a twist. Rather than innovate an incremental improvement, a particular product, or specific type of service, the assignment was to innovate a world-changing meta-solution that would utterly transform a particular domain of human endeavor. They had to choose one of three categories for innovation: health care, education, or finance. And then they had forty-five minutes to reinvent the way that category would work in the future. Forty-five minutes to change the world.

One more thing. For the first ten minutes, they were not allowed to talk. They had to draw, together. Why? Two reasons. First: talking can get circular really fast. Second: drawing (and you don't need to draw well for this to be true; in fact, the less comfortable you are drawing, the more effective it is) forces a different mode of thinking. It forces us out of what we know (words, sentences, established grammar, and thus established ideas) into the realm of imagination, because when we draw, we are literally envisioning. A silent conversation conducted through drawing gets things going more quickly than any kickoff discussion. It's all about speed.

The first thing they had to draw was what they thought the real, underlying problem is. Because too often, we jump into a brief without establishing what actually needs to be solved. For example, "Sales are down. We need to get a promotion out." But the real problem might not be sales messaging or pricing, it could be any number of things, from shelf position, lack of sales staff knowledge, or even a distribution logistics jam. Triple-clicking on any challenge to get to the real problem is going to be a key core competency in the Conscience Economy. You'd think this was a given in business today. It's not. The accelerated pace of decision making has too frequently eliminated thoughtful consideration.

An ironic statement, given that this is an innovation exercise that's all about speed. So, back to the save-the-world session. Once groups had drawn up their understanding of the real problem (which, I noted with interest, invariably had something to do with the systemic lack of access to critical information and resources—across the board, the teams felt that the core issue was an accessibility problem), it was time to draw up the solution, and this time they could talk. By now, they had a little more than half an hour.

Working quickly can be energizing, and to their surprise, everyone was able to imagine not only a game changer but concepts that were, in my estimation, technologically plausible.

Indeed, some of the solutions generated were so breathtaking that I should have had my patent lawyer sit in on the session. They invented a concept called Health Networking, an intuitive and even fun-to-use social network combining connected mobile diagnostics, personal experiences shared in real time, and collective resources. They invented a mobile application that transformed everyday life into a kind of virtual school, where challenging circumstances became lessons that were shared with a virtual community in the very context—the time and place—that the lesson would be most valuable and a positive outcome the most meaningful. And they invented a new kind of tradeable currency and credit system that assigns quantifiable value to accrued life experience, thus incentivizing people to improve themselves and others around them, thus increasing the value of everyone's currency account.

Ingredients and Modalities

Collective innovation is more than an open solicitation for opinions and advice. It means actively engaging others in the process of creating something new. It is not just a communications strategy (though by inviting others in, it will certainly achieve strategic communications goals). It is a great way to learn. And what emerges is nearly always thrilling. The process is as fruitful as the outcome.

Crowdifying

Crowdifying is virtual collaboration on a mass scale. As real-time social technology becomes a richer multimedia experience, and as videoconferencing overtakes static photography as a primary means of virtual telepresence, it will continue to be easier to catalyze, manage, and harvest and fund ideas from outside your business. Crowdifying is about more than ideas and opinions. It's also applicable to funding and generating utility content.

Crowdfunding is now a well-known means of generating investment for ideas that might not merit the attention of major investors, but for which individual consumers vote with their wallets. More than a means of helping businesses get off the ground, it's a harbinger of things to come—people willing to vote with their hard-earned cash for things that they think are meaningful or game-changing. By increasing the number of stakeholders in entrepreneurial success, crowdfunding by its very definition creates a communal sense of business opportunity and fiscal accountability. And it enables more people to have the experience—and in the best cases, the benefits—of being entrepreneurial investors.

Crowdsourcing will continue to evolve as a core technique for the creation of what I call "utility content"—useful, actionable, human-generated information. Particularly when embedded in mobile mapping and navigation, crowdsourced contributions will be the swiftest and most effective means of generating up-to-the-moment advice. For example, drivers can upload traffic or road conditions. Bicycle riders can contribute advice about the flattest, safest routes across town. Shoppers can share their discoveries. In the Conscience Economy, businesses will incentivize people to contribute their experiences, observations, desires, and discoveries to crowdsourced content utilities. The more people put in, the more useful the consolidated content. An "Internet of People" will be a vibrant and intelligent source of business value.

But crowdifying can happen within your business as well, not only to solve product problems but to monitor operational ethics, improve the environmental and social impact of your operations, and identify opportunities for value creation, efficiency, and growth.

Tinkering

It's now a basic expectation that technology, software, and even biology can be collectively hacked, invaded, meddled with, manipulated, broken down, reassembled, and rebuilt. Imagine creating your products or services with the express intention that they be in some sense hackable, reconfigurable, and able to be transformed for the better by the crowd. Hackability assumes that nothing is set in stone, that objects, information, and functionality are fluid and changeable. Tinkering as a collective impulse can be harnessed by business to improve processes, communications, products and services, and more. Wikis are classic examples of tinkering and collective adjusting to improve the end result.

Making

There's a renewed fascination with crafting, building, and making things, from the kitchen to the hardware bench. Young people are making their own beer, pickles, bikes, and companies. They exhibit an obsession with craftsmanship and quality. Is it a response to the technologicalization of everything? A physical-world version of self-empowerment?

Likely to become as accessible as printing ultimately became, 3D printing will bring a *Star Trek*–quality of physical object design and replication to a wider group of people. Perhaps the digitization of nearly everything in our lives has spawned a craving for getting hands-on again? 3D printing is set to re-localize elements of manufacture, particularly industrial product parts, but eventually customized consumer goods as well. How might your business provide products and solutions that help people make things—and not only dinner, but things like, say, schools or transit systems—together?

Collaborative Fixing

Buy, buy, buy, the current economic system shouts at us. How about fix, fix, fix? Could fixing be the new making? Not a return to the austerity of "make do and mend" but rather the mass adoption of repairing, upcycling, and repurposing for the thrill of it. Planned obsolescence runs counter to Conscience Economy values. It can be corrosive to brand trust. Product companies have an incentive not to get people to fix things and instead to buy more, but might fixing, upgrading, and sustaining be the new fabulous? Could emerging fixing communities become a platform for opportunities for profitable service extensions, cross-selling, and up-selling across your product portfolio?

Open source enables coders to fix things in the digital world. The next phase: hacking the physical world. Fixing things in the real world, whether shoes, or economic systems, is highly satisfying. Giving our favorite products a new life feels good, and can deepen our affection for a brand. Nudie Jeans picked up on this trend and created a free jeans repair program to bring new life to worn-out pairs—because jeans, as we all know, get better with age. But so do a lot of things. Fixing advice can be crowdsourced. iFixit.org—a fixing wiki—proclaims the arrival of "the repair revolution," stating without a wink of irony that "repair is freedom, repair creates jobs, repair is sustainable." Meanwhile, digitally enabled physical pop-ups like popuprepair.com build real-world community around taking care of—and thus giving a second life to—possessions we own, rely upon, and cherish. How might you enlist, certify, and incentivize a crowd of your fans to be your own distributed version of a Genius Bar?

Microtasking

The digitization and mobilization of work makes it possible to break many work-flow processes into distinct and separate tasks. Subdividing any goal into a set of miniaturized work tasks creates a set of modular ingredients, called microtasks, which can be distributed to a wide group of people and, once completed, be reconstituted and even reconfigured at will. From document translation (sentence by sentence) to the validation of basic data calculations and data points to the sharing of everyday

observations through digital photos or comments, broad and continuous initiatives—from data management to on-the-ground humanitarian aid—can be broken into microtasks and distributed to large groups
of people. CrowdFlower, one of several microtasking solutions, even
claims a "workforce" of seven million individuals. Microtasks can be
gamified—for example, the completion of a microtask can be built into
contests or offered as a purchase incentive. And they can transform how
work works.

The Power of Giving Up Power

Authorship is a kind of power, and by adopting collective innovation as a
strategic principle in your business, you are, in effect, sharing that power
with others. Giving up power is not the most comfortable thing to do,
especially for business leaders. But consider this: whether you actively let
go and open up your value-creation processes or not, customers will eventually find ways to break in. Collective innovation will be a rich source
of value growth, not only because it yields more robust customer-proven
solutions, but also because an engaged person—whether employee, customer, vendor, partner, or citizen—is automatically going to be more
loyal, more helpful, more valuable. When people feel they have a stake in
the innovation, they are more likely to promote it on your behalf.

Consider collective innovation as a guiding principle throughout your
organization, and make it part of your culture. Make room—in the budget as well as in your management protocols—for the possibility of failure, and ensure that you visibly celebrate risk taking. Some ways to get
started include the following:

- Start with the "what." Identify those areas of your enterprise in which
  collaborative innovation could be easily tested. Push your thinking—
  consider initiatives that might seem unlikely candidates for open collaboration, for example, employee incentives, an urgent competitive
  action, or a sales promotion.

- Next, determine the "how." What existing platforms can you leverage? How secure do they need to be, depending upon the nature
  of the initiative? You might need to build a secure and proprietary

environment, or you may be able to use third-party solutions and social media platforms. Make sure virtual collaboration platforms are high on the CTO agenda.

- Include collective innovation in the earliest stages of your product development process. Recruit teams of customers to cocreate product and service concepts with your innovation team, either in person or virtually.

- Start with a pilot project. Choose a specific initiative or object to collectivize, and use it to establish a scalable collaboration platform—whether that platform is digitally enabled or a physical, real-world process—that can be deployed on other projects across your business. It can be useful to start with a physical collaboration, learn from the process to specify platform requirements, and then virtualize.

- Try something ambitious: invite people from within and outside your business to address the world's toughest challenges under the umbrella of your brand and your offering. If you enlisted people to solve, say, mass unemployment, as members of your brand, what would they do? Use the output to guide the evolution as well as the positioning of your product offering.

- Promote a culture of collective innovation by actively and publicly endorsing the most breakthrough new ideas and the individuals and groups who developed them as often as you can—in leadership communication, in your marketing, across your communications, at point of sale.

In the Conscience Economy, business success requires an ever wider range of constituencies working together to build value—whether improving and optimizing processes, improving and innovating products and services, or delivering positive environmental and social impact. The interdependencies increase. Your business will rely on more interdependent and mutually accountable relationships than ever before. And that means it's time to rethink business accountability.

8

The New Accountability

The world situation is very serious. That must be apparent to all intelligent people. I think one difficulty is that the problem is one of such enormous complexity that the very mass of facts presented to the public by press and radio make it exceedingly difficult for the man in the street to reach a clear appraisement of the situation. Furthermore, the people of this country are distant from the troubled areas of the earth and it is hard for them to comprehend the plight and consequent reactions of the long-suffering peoples.

—GEORGE MARSHALL, Harvard University; June 5, 1947

The Marshall Plan, or as it was officially called, the European Recovery Program was as visionary as the secretary of state and Nobel Laureate who led its creation. General Marshall had experienced firsthand the human toll, environmental ravages, and economic destruction of world war. He spoke eloquently of a broken Europe, garnering support for policies that helped the region rebuild itself, in the full knowledge that this was more than a charitable act—it was pragmatic. Getting the European economy back on its feet was vital to America's own economic and national security interests. This is as true today as it ever was. Healthy economies everywhere are mutually dependent.

Here's the big difference today. We are no longer distant from the "plight and consequent reactions of the long-suffering peoples." Thanks to real-time digital media, we are closer to them than ever before. The person in the street can feel direct consequences from individual and corporate financial decisions, whether it's a product purchase, fuel consumption, or a company's worker safety record. A virtuous and unstoppable flywheel of cause and effect is gaining momentum; easier access to knowledge about enviro-social consequences has created a hunger for it, and this conscience-driven demand fuels the innovation of solutions that deliver even more access to knowledge and insight. With such awareness comes the expectation that business will be a positive force in the world. Every business will require its form of a Marshall Plan.

In 1970, Nobel Prize–winning economist and patron saint of free market capitalism Milton Friedman made a now iconic statement in the *New York Times*: "There is one and only one social responsibility of business—to use its resources and engage in activities designed to increase its profits **so long as it stays within the rules of the game, which is to say, engages in open and free competition without deception or fraud.**" (Emphasis mine.) Notice that even the laissez-faire Friedman acknowledged a degree of moral contract between the enterprise and its ecosystem.

I personally believe Friedman's statements were well intended, even if his comments, taken out of context, make him sound like a meanie to our ears in this, our supposedly more enlightened century. Friedman simply didn't believe it was the job of business to proactively and directly change society. He felt business should stay out of the way but play fair. When businesses played by the rules (and the rules were set by government) and focused on a singular motivation—profit—those entities that were purpose-built to solve social ills could get on with it.

What Friedman couldn't have imagined was the growing power of the citizen and the customer that the Internet would unleash across the world. ("He simply wasn't," says the CEO of an international technology provider with whom I'm debating economic theory, "a CMO.") Despite the social upheavals of the late 1960s, or perhaps because of them, it seemed rational and even starkly visionary to suggest that open and unregulated supply and demand would ultimately stabilize society by providing a fair and balanced economy. Consumer demand itself had yet to be informed by social empathy or environmental concerns. The world had yet to experience the media and activist magnification of massive and ecologically destructive corporate accidents along the lines of the Exxon Valdez or Bhopal disasters, probably all of which created mass outrage and contributed to the increased volume of a public call for more proactive corporate responsibility. He couldn't have imagined how virtual proximity to the suffering of others would invoke a sense of personal accountability for the purchases we make.

He certainly couldn't have predicted the spectrum of holistic social and environmental impact analysis tools that the global accountancy and financial reporting industries would be compelled to create. There's no question that the rules of the game Friedman refers to have changed.

The Conscience Economy will be more globally collaborative and participatory than any economic era that preceded it. This is not merely because it's easier than ever to jump in with an opinion, or because it feels good to flex our newfound digital and social empowerment. It's more collaborative because the world is more connected in real time than ever before. Business especially. The interdependencies and accountabilities that are the basis of productive enterprise are more clear to more people than ever before. We simply *know* more. And with that knowing comes an increased feeling of closeness to and responsibility for the well-being of others. This trajectory is set not only to continue but to accelerate.

Indeed, as many business leaders have already acknowledged, there is a revolution underway in the way financial performance is measured, not only in terms of the profitability, risk, and long-term value of the enterprise, but in assessing and tracking financial investments.

Measuring the consequences and outcomes of complex interactions between businesses, suppliers, transport, natural resources, communities, workers, and governments is no mean feat, especially given that much of the impact reveals itself more qualitatively. While the C-suite requires concise facts and bulletproof figures in order to make decisions, the correlations between qualitative results and financial business performance are, at best, fluctuating signals, because fluctuations in social and environmental circumstances (for example, a major storm, a factory accident, a change in political regime) shift social context, sense of urgency, and behavior. This much-talked-about era of continuous volatility that businesspeople are navigating is in no small part due to tightened interrelationships among all the factors that drive business growth. The more seemingly erratic the contingencies that impact value growth, the more unstable things seem.

I say "seem" because stability, of course, is relative. It's long past time to abandon any expectation for linear, predictable progress, comforting as the notion is. It is also long past time to abandon the debate between "pure" free market capitalism (which has never existed anyway) and government interventionist regulation. Adam Smith's "invisible hand" is no longer invisible. It has revealed itself. The invisible hand is *us*, the connected citizens of the world, held out metaphorically and digitally— thumbs up, thumbs down. We like, or we don't like, and we let everyone else know. We vote for the outcomes in which we most believe, not only with our voices but with our wallets.

Good Relationships

I fire up the BBC app on my iPhone to see the latest news from CES, the influential annual consumer electronics conference in Las Vegas, and the lead story catches my eye. Intel, the world's largest chip manufacturer, has just announced to the world that in 2014, all the chips it ships will be "conflict free." CEO Brian Krzanich is urging the "entire industry" to follow suit.

To be fair, Intel is not the first electronics manufacturer to sound the alarm on "conflict minerals," which traditionally include gold, tungsten, tin, and tantalum. Indeed, Nokia, Apple, HP, and most major global electronics manufacturers have signed on to the OECD (Organisation for Economic Co-operation and Development) protocols as part of their membership in the Electronic Industry Citizenship Coalition.

Still, what's astonishing to me is not the drama of the announcement itself, but that it garners significant column inches in the highly competitive tech news category. Microchips have joined the crusade for societal betterment. This represents a new phase of business logic: the mainstreaming of societal values manifest through business.

It will come as no surprise that I am unabashedly delighted about the increasing social zeal among business leaders, but for all the encouraging signs, I cannot shake a nagging curiosity about how business leaders rationalize this priority to their boards. When I mention this to a friend over a coffee, she says, "Talk to Kevin Murray—he's been involved in this work for decades."

Kevin is both an author of two books on leadership and the chairman and CEO of the aptly named Good Relations Group, a company that offers a portfolio of services including C-level leadership coaching, strategic advisory services, and brand and public communications.

We meet on a chilly day in his office in Central London, a view of dour-looking gray Edwardian office buildings in the background. But our conversation quickly takes us far from the wintry murkiness to a bright and hopeful South Africa, where Kevin is from and where his career began as a journalist for a newspaper with an editorial point of view opposed to apartheid government. There were police visitations, banned stories, threats "During the Soweto riots," Kevin says, "we went into the township, hidden in the trunk of a car that followed the police in. You fool yourself into thinking you're actively doing something, but actually you're just reporting." But one of the things he found himself increasingly reporting on was the growing trend of businesses making decisions that were counter to apartheid law. "It was," he reflects, "the only practical thing to do for business."

The eventual overthrow of apartheid, in no small part due to pressures exerted on the government by global businesses, changed Kevin's life and career. He became a convert to "the whole idea that business could be a force for good."

He moved from the newspaper into reporting for corporate and trade publications, which eventually led him into the belly of the beast: working in strategy and communications directly for some rather "controversial" industries (his word, not mine), including big pharma and nuclear energy. "Having to go out and talk to local communities on behalf of a business, and relate to their concerns about building a plant that could put toxic chemical fumes into their immediate environment—that's front-end relationship building. It's genuine and palpable. And at the end of the day, the only way people would let you do anything is if they trusted you," says Kevin.

Corporations touch—and thus can either hurt, or help—so many people, whether employees, partners, suppliers, customers, vendors, or citizens and community members. "It's not about stakeholders," Kevin finally says to me, "it's about relationships." Just that simple shift in language suggests a more human and conscientious approach to business.

Stakeholder management, as Kevin says, is rational, while relationships are emotional. The corporation has the power to take a stand, establish cultural biases and moral value systems, and deploy them to deepen trust and improve the effectiveness of these relationships. I ask him if this is all a bit too fuzzy for the hard-nosed business executive to stomach. He smiles. "What's the total value of all listed companies? Sixty trillion dollars? How much of that value is intangible?" He's referring to things like customer loyalty, brand value, future earnings potential, risk profiles. "I believe $30 trillion of global business's worth is in what I'd call soft capital. And no one wants a deficit in soft capital. Trust has a real monetary value and directly impacts cash flow."

Trust, as a multiyear Global Monitor study completed by Kantar's Futures Company shows, indeed has monetary value. A 1 percent increase in trust—as evidenced by customers' stated perceptions of both a company's reputation and behavior, and their feelings about brands—can generate a 3 percent increase in business value. This increase is attributable to such things as consistency of repurchase, the increased success of up-selling and cross-selling, and the effects of consumer advocacy.

But the current trust trends should be worrying, because globally, trust in corporations is going down, not up, according to Kantar's year-on-year research. Seventy-one percent of consumers worldwide believe that companies will take advantage of them if they feel they won't be found out. The most trusted category of business—surprisingly, this is the tech sector—enjoys a 43 percent level of trust. That means that nearly 60 percent of people surveyed worldwide state that they don't trust companies in the sector. The least trusted category—banking—has just a 6 percent trust level. Meanwhile people's sense of agency—the impact they can have through the choices they make—is on a year-on-year rise. Sixty-four percent of people worldwide believe that they can "make a difference in the world around me" through their purchases and actions. In the U.S., that figure jumps to 73 percent. While there's clear decay in trust, the sense of agency—and the willingness to act—is on the rise.

Business is ultimately a network of human relationships. Some of these fall into the category of first-level, or first-order, relationships: those people who directly interact with or work for an organization and are directly impacted by its operations. These include employees, citizens, customers, investors, vendors, and even key competitors. First-order relationships have been on the radar for some time. But in our hyper-connected world, second-order relationships are of increasing importance. These relationships are indirect, and experience second-order impact. They include local communities, employees of suppliers, suppliers to suppliers, governments, local institutions like schools and hospitals, and fellow industry colleagues. In a hyperconnected world, these relationships are of increasing importance. And they can be more difficult to track. But it's not impossible.

Measuring the Immeasurable

The classic Six Sigma adage "If you don't measure it, it doesn't get done" gets a slight semantic makeover in the Conscience Economy: in order to manage it, you need to monitor it. The Conscience Economy business needs a new dashboard. Future-proof businesses must reconsider and redesign their accountability infrastructure.

The paradigm of the "economic externality" is being turned on its head. In the Conscience Economy, externality becomes materiality. To put it in layman's terms, everything a business does matters. It all impacts the bottom line.

In the Conscience Economy, a business commits to being environmentally and socially sensible for a host of reasons: because business relies on limited and often fragile natural and social capital that must be managed; because the practice exceeds customer expectations; because it is brand differentiating and builds trust; because it provides a guiding mission for innovation; because it attracts and engages talent; and, ultimately, because it's the right thing to do. The new reality of operational interdependence, resource fragility, and individual empowerment means that doing what's best for the whole business ecosystem (which includes natural and social capital) is just how it's done. The correlation of environmentally and socially sensible business practices with profit is set to become a given, although the levers will be different depending upon your offering. In the Conscience Economy, as a business, you must sustain profitability, but never at the expense of social or environmental outcomes.

An historic example of businesses aligning to take accountability for social progress came in 1977, when a consortium of global businesses signed onto the Sullivan Principles, created by an American theologian. This act put pressure on the South African apartheid government to abandon the injustice of its system. But what about things going the other way? Business can impact good, in clearly measurable ways. But can good impact business in a comparably measurable way?

Establishing a link between conscientious business practice and profitability has long been, as you can imagine, the holy grail for CSR professionals and corporate idealists. The quest for a holistic set of standards began in earnest in the 1980s, when CSR was becoming professionalized. For decades, practitioners have combed through numbers, looking for correlations that prove a quantifiably defensible case for good corporate citizenship.

As the CSR discipline was ascending, this quest made perfect sense, because intuition would suggest doing good is simply good business, and good business should be profitable. Meanwhile, no department—particularly one with such missionary zeal for changing the world—wants to be perceived as a nice-to-have function but, ultimately, a cost center. However, quantifying intangibles in the same way that we can quantify hard assets—no matter how intuitively we may feel there is a value in those intangibles—is a notoriously tricky prospect, not least because most boardrooms aren't exactly hospitable environments for qualitatively sourced evidence. Hard quantitative evidence—the kind you can break down and add—is the universal language of business accountability. Counting is what ultimately counts.

The problem is, counting looks backward, not ahead. Counting is something you do after the big decisions have been made. How much product is still in the warehouse? How much sold? How much didn't? How much cash is in the bank? How many employees are on the payroll? If counting were an accurate predictor of future business success and not just an assessment of past performance, then theoretically, no big business would ever fail unless it truly botched on execution. Of course, we know that great big hairy intangibles—like sudden shifts in consumer expectations—are what ultimately drive customer demand, the "utility" motivation that underpins all current economic theories. That which is hardest to count or hardest to measure is also that which is most fundamental to the assessment of future business performance.

Meanwhile, for the last ten years, the meme of "true cost economics" has been gaining ground. A manifesto propelled itself onto the web around 2005, proclaiming the necessity of calculating the hard financial costs of environmental and social consequences of business production—and converting the results of the calculation into corporate tax liability. However that makes you feel, it's worth noting that the idea has steadily moved from the progressive sidelines into mainstream conversations—not only in academia, but across the accounting industry—about financial accountability, particularly as it relates to mitigating future risk and creating more stable growth forecasts. In the future, smart businesses will track a wide range of costs and benefits that are consequent with its various operations and strategic decisions, in addition to its bottom line. These might include, for example, environmental impact and its potential to augment or compromise profits as well as workforce well-being and its impact on near-term productivity. The ultimate intent: a more accurate picture of both the current and future bottom line.

What if we've been looking at measurement principles from the wrong angle? The very search for a pattern of correlation between improved corporate citizenship and a rise in profit implies that doing good is an "add-on," a "nice-to-have" incremental investment of time and resource. An enterprise initiates a program that diminishes negative environmental impact, and then it asks, "Was it worth it?" as it looks for evidence of a correlating rise in profitability or value share.

This, the typical approach to measurement and reporting, is firmly entrenched in looking back on the comfortable certainties (even if they depict uncomfortable truths) of past performance. It's the proverbial driving-by-looking-in-the-rearview-mirror. It's a well-used crutch. Metrics illustrating past performance are used to rationalize decisions. Too often, measurement gets in the way of understanding rather than enriching it. Nassim Nicholas Taleb has famously stated that the past is no accurate predictor of the future. In the Conscience Economy, business expends the bulk of its energy looking forward, using a real-time dashboard of analytics that support its mission to do its part in making the world better for all humanity. Just as an actual dashboard shows when we've breached the speed limit, the new accountability dashboard will show when we've begun to do harm.

What every future-proof business needs is a *redesigned accountability infrastructure.*

That infrastructure includes a clear map of the relationships that are being tracked and forecast, a set of tools for monitoring performance and making business decisions, and a reporting framework for upholding accountability to customers, investors, employees, and indeed, everyone else.

Dimensions of Accountability

You won't be starting from scratch: when it comes to measuring and monitoring social and environmental impact, the challenge is not one of scarcity but rather one of overabundance. Indeed, once you start looking, there are an almost overwhelming number of industry associations, reporting pilot projects, codes of conduct, political affiliations, certification standards, and analytical frameworks. None is perfect. All are works in progress. Several openly compete for legitimacy. Regional variations of enforcement methods are generally linked to regional cultural stereotypes—er, norms—i.e., the Europe-based associations bake in strong government involvement, while North American–founded alliances and certifying bodies place the power of enforcement in the hands of businesses themselves.

Here's an example of a quibble between two business citizenship alliances in the apparel industry that would be humorous if the circumstances that gave rise to them weren't so serious. In 2013 the Rana Plaza factory collapse in Bangladesh, which killed more than 1,100 people, catalyzed nearly all the mainstream "fast fashion" retailers in Europe to sign the Accord on Fire and Building Safety in Bangladesh, stating that they won't condone manufacturing in unsafe conditions and will directly involve themselves in safety inspection. April 24, the anniversary of the tragedy, has even been declared Fashion Revolution Day by an international consortium, with impressive marketing support and publicity. Are these initiatives signifying accountability or savvy brand building? It's the fashion business, after all.

These kinds of responses to what is inarguably inhumane may sound good to the general public and generate positive press, but it's tough to live up to in the often more byzantine business systems of developing economies. Differing concepts of accountability, corruption, and governance make it challenging to monitor and enforce even the most strict and well-intentioned codes of conduct. North American companies like Walmart and Gap refused to sign the European document, creating their own accord for the Alliance for Bangladesh Worker Safety, which, according to the Europeans, lacks legally binding accountability, relying instead on the goodwill of the business itself to uphold the principles of the accord. In time, however, citizens and their wallets will be the enforcing body. The tragedy of compromising worker safety in the interest of cost savings are as old as industry itself, but the noise level is rising, and it's becoming front and center for people.

Today, market research suggests that although people find these stories appalling and expect business to do something about them, most are unwilling to make a sacrifice—and this includes paying a higher price—for badness-free products. And you know what? I wouldn't either. The key here is the statement "pay more." Why should we? Shouldn't conscientious business operations be a given? I know no business leader who wouldn't agree that worker safety is a business responsibility, not an add-on.

Still, Primark, one of the world's leading "fast fashion" retailers, has seen profits rise by 14 percent in the year since the disaster. It's tough to reconcile competitive pricing pressure with the cost of safer business practice, at least today. Passing on the cost of conscientious business practice to the customer, unless you're a luxury brand built upon the margin of meaning, is likely to backfire. But in the Conscience Economy, the cost of environmentally and socially sensible business practices is likely to fall as new technologies make conscientious operations easier and more efficient. For example, "near-shoring" and even "re-shoring" manufacturing is on its way, eliminating some of the current challenges with enforcement of codes of conduct.

The ability to enforce is the biggest issue when it comes to holistic accountability, particularly when it comes to suppliers that operate in cultures with radically different value systems around health, safety, and physical infrastructure. The undeniable reality is that cheap manufacturing environments are rarely situated in high-functioning, low-corruption democracies. Supplier codes of conduct are tougher to enforce than those at a company's own factories. But the combination of market demand with new, connected monitoring tools and technologies—coupled with innovation that generates new manufacturing capabilities that increase efficiency and lower cost—will take friction out of the process. Progress toward holistic, trackable, enforceable accountability will be unstoppable, because it will be driven by the ultimate source of value—human motivation.

Reporting Frameworks

Despite the proliferation of different techniques and methodologies for measurement, three terms have risen to the top of the pile in the quest for a consistent approach to categorizing and analyzing metrics: triple bottom line; ESG, which stands for environmental, social, governance; and integrated reporting. Every business leader across every function should be as conversant in these three concepts as they are in profit and loss.

Triple bottom line typically refers to an *internal* enterprise accounting framework that acknowledges real-cost economics. In other words, it includes the environmental and social costs of company operations as part of the balance sheet. "People, planet, profit" is an easy mnemonic device for remembering what the triple stands for. Companies that ascribe to the triple bottom line concept pay at least passing attention to their environmental and social contribution in their financial reporting, although triple bottom line is largely a term and a philosophy, rather than a standardized methodology.

ESG is a term that refers to a data gathering and reporting framework used by impact investors and those assembling and tracking vehicles like ethical or environmentally focused mutual funds. The concept of ESG is more commonly used when assessing company performance across these dimensions from the outside, but the categorization can also be applied internally.

Integrated reporting is simultaneously a reporting framework, an analytical methodology, and a movement in the global accountancy field. It's a buzzy, and I'd even say chic, term; drop it into conversation with your CFO or your accountancy firm and see what happens. The integrated reporting movement aims for integrated reporting to be adopted as the global standard for financial reporting with near missionary zeal.

Born out of the aforementioned concept of true cost economics, an integrated report includes not only a holistic set of costs associated with the environmental and social consequences of business operations, but also includes assessments of future innovation potential, the stability of future resources, the well-being of employees—essentially, all the components that provide a picture of the overall health of the enterprise. It has emerged from an impressive coalition of companies participating in a pilot of its framework, and is facilitated by an international professional organization called the International Integrated Reporting Council (IIRC).

If you'd like to speak like a Conscience Economy native, know that these three terms can be used interchangeably. As in "Our business is driven by the triple bottom line. We're proud of our track record on ESG issues, and we'll be including them in our first quarterly integrated report."

Industry Alliances

A host of well-intentioned and sometimes even visionary industry alliances and coalitions are a potentially effective means of driving conscientious change. Your business may already be a member of such an alliance; the question is, is it a checked box or is it representative of your business's truest intent? Membership in the best of these organizations requires more than a subscription fee; in order to be impactful, the business must commit to the creation and deployment of a "management system" that ensures compliance with stated goals of the coalition. Management systems include such requirements as the assignment of accountable individuals within your organization, clearly stated objectives for improvement, regular documentation and reporting, audits, and procedures for corrective action should goals not be met or violations occur. For example, the initiative for conflict-free minerals that Intel so proudly advocates is a product of one such alliance, the EICC—the Electronic Industry Citizenship Coalition.

Codes of Conduct

Another modality for establishing at least the basis for and intent of Conscience Economy business accountability is *codes of conduct* authored by individual companies or agreed to by a set of signatories to a coalition. Whether a business chooses to go it alone or join the force of a broader alliance, codes of conduct establish useful principles not only for reporting, but for making strategic, enviro-socially sensible management decisions. They are usually emotionally stirring documents replete with imagery of healthy forests and well-cared-for workers. They read like the American Bill of Rights, but because they span transnational boundaries, they are theoretically only enforceable through contractual agreements with local suppliers. They can overcome local custom, but not local law. They can, however, exert pressure, and indeed, are a core weapon in enlightened business's fight to make the world fairer and more amendable to the innovation that accompanies democracy and personal liberty. A simple Google search will pull up nearly any publicly traded company's supplier code of conduct, just as the corporate website features a page on core values. In the Conscience Economy, such codes of conduct will become ever more front and center as statements of a business's value system made manifest in its operational approach. Indeed, these codes will be a key tool for matchmaking not only customers with brands and products, but for incentivizing innovation for social good.

Measurement Tools

The field of impact investing has yielded some of the most sophisticated trackers and metrics in the space, because by definition, impact investing is "pure" Conscience Economy. Its very existence is to drive positive and sustainable change while upholding the highest standards of reporting accuracy. Indeed, it's pragmatic for tools from the field of impact investing to be deployed within the enterprise as part of management decision making.

Impact investing as a growing category has begun to adopt more broadly accepted standards and principles. Currently, commonly used reporting standards with impressive lists of signatories include the social and environment risk-management framework called the Equator Principles; the Impact Reporting and Investment Standards (IRIS) put forth by the Global Impact Investing Network; and the Principles for Responsible Investment, which were established and ratified by the United Nations.

I have no incentive to push any particular company's portfolio, but as of this writing, one of the most complete suites of proprietary investment analysis tools is provided by MSCI; these tools provide a broad range of proprietary indices for investors to customize, based on performance benchmarks in relation to a range of ESG issues, from weighting companies based upon a positive environmental record to excluding companies involved in human rights abuses or even the manufacture of "controversial weapons."

If you don't regularly research investments by screening for particular aspects of a company's operations, you will find MSCI's website an eye opener. Indeed, the list of screens offered for filtering their research would look right at home on an ironic hipster tee shirt. But it's anything but ironic. You might even find it slightly unnerving. It goes straight to a wide range of values—some of them polarizing—that many people hold close.

"Clients can set screens on any degree of involvement in these businesses, or set revenue thresholds:

- Abortifacients
- Abortion Provider
- Adult Entertainment
- Alcohol
- Animal Welfare
- Cluster Bombs
- Contraceptives
- Firearms
- Gambling
- Genetic Engineering (GMOs)
- Land mines
- Nuclear Power
- Pork
- Predatory Lending and CRA Research
- Stem Cell
- Tobacco
- Weapons Producers"

And so on. It got me thinking—as it should you—about the many potential positives of big data, particularly the conscientious application of business and operational intelligence. If investors today can screen companies for any degree of involvement with *pork*, consumers will soon be able to screen for anything that matters to them.

In the Conscience Economy, the effectiveness of an ecosystem of inter-dependent accountabilities is not only more business-critical—explicitly demonstrating the impact of your actions on each of these accountabilities is vital. The conscientious company sees itself as equally answerable to more constituencies than ever before. Today, the new accountability remains a choice for enlightened organizations and leaders. But tomorrow, it will be as much a business requirement as profit itself. In South Africa, listed companies are already legally required to submit an integrated report on a "comply or explain" basis. And the global accountancy field is beginning to adapt its offering to address the growing demand from investors for visibility into longer-term financial performance, and factors including environmental and social capital are indicators of stable growth.

There's no question about it: it's hard work to engage and support a complex and interdependent ecosystem of relationships to achieve customer delight, profit, and measurable enviro-social impact. Indeed, a common CEO complaint, when confronted with the range of relationships and accountabilities that should be considered not only for quarterly reporting but regular management decision making, is, "That's creating more work."

But a blend of sensors, smart monitoring, improved quantitative data integration, and real-time qualitative feedback delivered through automated systems as well as social media will make it not only possible, but easier, to construct new management dashboards. As more operational processes become digital and therefore trackable, new analytics will laterally correlate performance outcomes of a broad range of business factors, from customer satisfaction and advocacy to pricing elasticity to environmental and social impact.

Good Intentions

Like any step in a new direction, it all starts with intent. In his work with C-suite executives, Kevin Murray has observed "a new wave of leader, ready to make bold decisions about social and environmental issues." Such a leader has a clear vision for the proactive role her business can play in improving human life, society, and the environment.

In other words, before you dive in and build your Conscience

Economy business dashboard, establish your business's accountability principles. Is accountability only a means of managing employees and satisfying shareholders, or are you committed to satisfying a broader array of relationships? You make the commitment to monitoring more than just the traditional bottom line, and you commit to reporting on what you monitor.

Every organizational culture is unique—some organizations are highly fact driven, while others place a high degree of trust in intuition. It's up to you to determine not only what you measure, but how measurement is used, and specifically how it factors into forward-looking business decisions.

Get started. Establish a task force for building a new accountability dashboard. Do not consign it solely to the office of the CFO. The new accountability crosses all functions, and cross-functional participation is vital, because increased cross-functional information sourcing will be at the heart of monitoring, forecasting, and reporting.

- Go straight to your vision. What is your most conscientious objective? Based upon that, catalogue the key dimensions you'll need to observe, measure, forecast, and understand.

- Assess your current culture of measurement. Every organization has one. Be brutally honest with yourself: is it a means of rationalizing a decision after the fact, a guide to future choices, a check in the box, a go or no-go gateway for all decisions?

- Map your key accountabilities and relationships. Sort them by first order—those constituencies you directly engage—and second order—those who are not directly engaged but are indirectly affected by your operations. Encourage line employees to catalogue their relationships inside and outside the business as well.

- Identify natural and civic resources that your business uses, impacts, or could help restore.

- Correlate existing industry bodies, monitoring, and certification benchmarks and standards with each of these relationships. If you aren't already, get involved in them. Do not consign this to a CSR department. Assign each member of your leadership team sponsorship of a particular accountability.

• Invite people from the range of external relationships you've mapped to tell you how they'd like your performance to be assessed. How will they be assessing you as a corporate citizen?

• Prototype your own "integrated reporting" scorecard and conduct your own internal pilot.

• Assign a rock star statistician to create a proprietary predictive index that correlates the measurable success of specific conscientious initiatives with an increase in customer trust, engagement, loyalty, and sales.

• Establish principles for how your integrated reporting scorecard drives not only operational strategy and daily execution, but promotional communication and employee incentives.

• Don't fear the "soft stuff"—the qualitative, observation-based, and intuitive information. It can be the most powerful.

Even in the Conscience Economy, no business will ever be perfect. But the quality of your business relationships can be measurably improved by transparency about your intent and your progress toward achieving it.

A final and vital note: the outcome should not be reams of reports and presentations full of stats. Ultimately, the convergence of new trackable accountabilities can and should tell a powerful and motivating story. Involve communications talent—it's probably in your marketing department—who can find meaning in the figures and translate it into a story people can understand and use in their everyday decisions.

Business operates in the service of human lives. Life generates infinite data. But life is not made of data. Life is made of experiences, sensations, and emotions. Of course the facts matter. But only when you put them in a meaningful context. Thus, stories are always more effective than stats. Because stories are more human.

9

What You See Is What You Get

It's a new day, and rush hour is underway. In cities everywhere, the expanded bikeways are bustling with riders on their morning commutes, while an increasing proportion of electric cars whizz along the freeways. Across the globe, vastly expanded and energy-efficient public transit systems that intelligently address capacity based on passenger flow are full of riders on superfast Internet connections, enjoying media, watching the news, playing games, or catching up on work. A business executive studies an energy balance report to see how much power his company's solar panels have put back into the grid this week. A student in a prestigious international virtual university is playing a multiuser networked game that improves her leadership skills. A new grandmother makes faces at her infant grandson halfway across the world.

Drivers reenergize their electric cars and their mobile devices at small, efficient, and convenient charging spaces, while smart thermostats and energy meters silently and swiftly exchange information across the Internet of Things, winding down consumption in balance with weather and conditions as people leave—and enter—their homes and offices. A combination of intelligent-system capacity management and the discovery and increasing affordability of new sources of energy, as well as incentives for saving and trading it between people and organizations, makes electricity a more abundant resource than it has ever been before.

Fresh, healthy food is also abundant. The sun shines brightly on broad patchworks of localized urban farms conveniently positioned within city greenbelts and on reclaimed land. The harvests they produce are delivered to local markets and shops, and are augmented by fresh imports from overseas, delivered in bulk, maximizing not only the price efficiency of economies of scale, but also energy efficiency, a fact that appears in labeling so consumers can consider it as they make their choices.

Biofuels grow on reclaimed brownfields, and subarctic boreal pine forests are preserved, nurtured, and spread ever further south, to encourage their global-warming-fighting aerosols to flourish. Biodiversity of flora and the fauna they support—insects, small animals, birds—spread into cities and suburbs, in parks, in yards, on rooftops, ensuring not only a more pleasant environment for everyday life, but supporting and sustaining the planet's overall ecosystem.

Recycling becomes more automatic, efficient, and local, returning commodity materials like paper to economically viable, inexpensive, disposable, and reusable resources.

Even recycled water becomes commonplace, with common standards of gradation known by all: water for cleaning, water for growing, water for drinking. Advances in desalination, powered by wave energy and solar energy, drive resurgent oceanfront economies, and agribusiness expands into the deserts.

Re-shored and re-localized manufacturing stimulates economic growth everywhere, minimizes fuel consumption, and puts consumer-centric design in direct proximity with manufacturing, creating a virtuous cycle of continuous product and operational improvement. Smaller-scale factories and workshops are integrated with virtualized education and wellness programs, ensuring the vitality, well-being, and subsequent productivity and loyalty of their local workforce.

Videoconferencing is portable, and it's everywhere. Virtual presence and virtual intimacy have made collaboration across time and space nearly effortless, much less expensive, and in some cases even more effective than being together in person, because diverse teams can not only bring multiple perspectives, but multiple and simultaneous contexts to the table.

The evaporation of privacy has reversed course. Companies compete to deliver the most privacy and the greatest security as they depend ever more on constant connection to customers. Peer-to-peer networking has become ubiquitous, meaning no one ever needs to rely on solely traditional network subscriptions in order to be connected. Network operators become peer-to-peer facilitators.

As human rights spread successfully across the globe, the issue of data rights emerges as a new battleground. Data about each person is available to him or her, and companies encourage people to access and use it on their own behalf. The data-mining script has flipped—the power of big data is in the hands of individuals who choose when and where to share who they are and what their needs are, to attract companies, brands, and products that meet their needs.

Customers vote with their wallets, their purchases, and their voices on social media, sanctioning those products, services, and companies that best represent their own values, because it's easier than ever before to understand the connection between their choices and the impact those choices have on their world. Most people buy less stuff than they once did, but invest instead in rich experiences that enhance the thrill of being alive. From restaurants to sports to learning and even investing, experiences are what people value, seek out, remember, brag about. Travel increases, but not just to relax and decompress. People increasingly travel to learn, to make new friends, to help restore communities, to give something back, to add meaning to their lives, and to gain status among their friends. This last one—status—may seem out of step with conscientiousness. But in fact it's key to it. Adventurous, life-enhancing experiences (not unlike philanthropy) are on the rise as desirable signifiers of social status, and social status is one of the core motivations driving the Conscience Economy. Conscience, after all, is social.

Sensors on wearable smart devices continuously monitor personal biometrics, transmitting vital information directly to physicians, pharmacists, wellness coaches, nutritionists, and other health-care providers, taking strain off the system and making better health accessible to more people than ever before. Through social media, patients share experiences and advice in real time, forming larger alliances to give them health-care purchasing power and to lobby health providers for innovative and improved treatment options. Because so many health-care processes are disintermediated through mobile biosensors, a continuous stream of diagnostic information, and improved automation, doctors, nurses, and patients are able to be closer than ever before when it really matters, whether in person or through videoconferencing.

People no longer feel the need to always be plugged in, as intelligent automation makes it possible for online profiles and processes to temporarily self-manage while we disconnect. Everyday connected technology is less invasive, more glanceable, and easier to time shift. The culture places a high value on mindfulness, physical presence, and the pleasure of live experience. The new etiquette requires being physically and totally present with others in the moment. There are even establishments that prohibit connectivity and facilitate unplugging.

Elite luxury brands in fashion, automotive, food, and hospitality continue to represent the extremes of our aspirations, which now include sustainability and ethical production, fuel efficiency, and alternative energy. Sustainable and ecologically aspirational five-star resorts attract guests who enjoy the temporary and highly curated experience of living in balance with the world without any sense of compromise; rather, it feels like a luxurious and aspirational privilege. Recirculated water for endless hot showers is fresh and clean. Hydroponic food is grown so locally that it's harvested from rooftops—it is picked off the plant and prepared before your eyes by a chef and his students who are participating in a training program that provides them with professional skills. Fashion is ethically sourced and produced, reintroducing and increasing the market value of quality and, increasingly, local craftsmanship. The most prestigious cars are more fuel efficient than ever before, combining advanced engineering with built-in intelligence. Fine wines are dry farmed and biodynamic. Cuisine is not only based on organic and local ingredients but produced as part of a nutritional or career education program, helping formerly disadvantaged people get on their feet. But aspirational and conscientious luxury extends beyond its traditional categories, encompassing bicycles, home appliances, and more.

Alternative forms of ownership, sharing, and value exchange have given rise to new and sometimes temporary currencies. Money is no longer the only way people trade. Buying is simply one way of getting something. Sharing and trading—cars, living spaces, skills—is enabled by new branded services that empower people to personalize the value they place on things and experiences.

Business ethics and conscientious operations are a purchase driver, as access to information has made citizens everywhere aware of costs they ultimately carry on behalf of business. From conflict-free sourcing to environmental restoration, ethical certification bodies are augmented by customers, citizens, and workers themselves, who can effortlessly contribute their observations and experiences of company behavior and facilities, creating real-time process and safety monitoring. Supplier codes of conduct, once difficult to enforce, become self-sustaining as information supplied by both connected sensors and human beings makes monitoring easier.

Everyday philanthropy—automatically giving to others by buying a product or subscribing to a service—has become a natural and, to some individuals, even a competitive instinct. Brands compete to integrate the sexiest and most impactful—and brag-worthy—acts of generosity into their product offerings. Meanwhile, brand activism—business using its economic leverage to influence hot public issues from human rights to health—has made the world's leading brands into heroes of the mass movement for good.

Everyone is empowered to be both teacher and student, mentor and protégé. Mass education is a hot new form of mass media. Sharing information, advice, and learnings from personal and professional life experience is not only a popular pastime, it's built into employee development programs, mass education, and even shopping scenarios. A customer immediately learns how others have deployed a service before she subscribes, and once she's in, she has a range of mentors who help her get the most out of it. A young entrepreneur in Latin America can learn in real time from a successful mentor in Scandinavia. The exchange of knowledge not only produces business value for the learner, it produces social credit and status for the teacher.

In the Conscience Economy, all business activity contributes to a global, upward spiral. Contributing goodness into society is not just about reputation management, risk mitigation, or cause marketing. Contributing goodness opens up new markets for talent, innovation, and customers. It stabilizes those markets and enables them to grow. It protects and strengthens that which business requires in order to exist: people and resources. Goodness is a wellspring of profit itself.

Wanting It

The Conscience Economy is no guarantee. We have to want it, and we have to work for it. When you boil it all down, there are two ways things could go. One scenario—the one where we let things proceed without a visionary intent to steer our world toward safety—is pretty ominous. The other is enlightened and encouraging, a world we'd be proud to say we'd done our part to usher in. A world that we'd be gratified to hand to future generations.

Perception shapes reality. What is yours? Is your glass of we're-running-out-of-water half empty? Do you see a scenario where it all goes wrong—widening gaps between rich and poor, new diseases, new conflicts, polar meltdown, and more? Or is your glass of desalinated, mineral-rich recycled water half full? Do you see increasing quality and length of life, emerging technologies and alternative energy sources, new value systems, and an unprecedented opportunity to make things better?

Concern about potentially catastrophic global outcomes has catalyzed a shift. But optimism is what will ultimately fuel the transformation of our world, and business success within it. It all starts with belief in possibility. What we see is what we'll get.

But it will mean defying certain aspects of our nature as human beings. A close friend recently took a daylong wilderness survival course. She's the last person I would have expected to do such a thing, as she's more Four Seasons than four-wheel drive. But she's also inherently curious, and although I too am unlikely to find myself lost in the woods (at least literally—metaphorically, I'm game) she eagerly shared with me one of the most surprising things she learned on her night in the wilds of Northern California's Marin Headlands.

It's about what you do first if you find yourself lost in the wilderness. Before you do anything else, you seek—or build—shelter, relief from the elements of cold, heat, and weather. Essentials like water and food come after—you can survive for a bit without them, but not without shelter.

This is ancient obviousness. We evolved to stay alive, and more often than not, staying alive is about putting a roof over our heads and keeping it there. It's about going with the flow, staying aligned with values of your community. Not sticking out. Not taking risks. It perhaps goes without saying that the best course of action is to avoid getting lost in the wilderness in the first place.

But most of us also intuitively know that continual risk avoidance is not only impossible, but that it invites other dangers. "All progress," as the eminently PowerPointable George Bernard Shaw quote goes, "depends upon the unreasonable man"—and woman, I'd add. In other words, as a society, we need people who have resisted the impulses of millennia of evolutionary adaptation. In order for society to move forward, we need people who resist the genetically circumscribed allure of safety. "I know this," you're thinking, "but I just don't want it to be me." Yup.

What a delicious paradox: we are born to seek safety and comfort by sticking with what we know, and yet ultimately, our safety and comfort require at least some people to push beyond the boundaries of what's safe and comfortable.

And so it's a relief that, as with all things human, there are indeed exceptions to the keep-your-head-down norm. There are people who seem to make audacity a way of life. Adrenaline junkies and rogue traders, for example. They boldly break out of norms, make high-risk decisions on a regular basis, and swagger through newspapers and business media. But more often than not, we learn of these individuals when the consequences of their actions have caused newsworthy harm. And thus, in the news and through popular memes, we are reminded that many of these individuals put their physical well-being, their families, and entire organizations in harm's way via their personal bias for going against the grain. The perils of derring-do are continually reinforced.

There are of course heroic exceptions too—Rosa Parks and her society-shaking bus ride come to mind. For good reason, we idolize Nelson Mandela, Steve Jobs, every Nobel Prize winner. No matter what our personal belief system, every one of us either consciously or subconsciously maintains an inner hagiology, a list of iconic people who inspire us.

We especially admire those heroes who push social values and behaviors into the realm of greater fairness for all. We put them on pedestals because they are not like the rest of us. For religious people, these pioneers may even be seen as divine. It's like we just know, deep inside, that true heroes are fundamentally different from normal people. Because in general, we human beings just aren't designed to be risk takers.

Seismic Instability

Rarer even than an individual risk taker is an organization willing to truly lean forward into the unseeable and unknown.

Even the seemingly agile and unstoppable Silicon Valley new elite tend to focus on what they know, on the more familiar and comfortable terrain of "digital disruption." What appears to be radical West Coast risk taking is often simply (and admirably) an operational model that follows prescribed ideologies and behavioral patterns within a highly regionalized and contextually specific culture. In the innovation centers of the world, those cities and regions with a far higher-than-average number of well-funded start-ups, it is normal to disrupt, to digitize, to virtualize, to fund, to have unwavering faith in an ever more digital tomorrow—and the wealth-generating valuation that will come with it.

But these beliefs and behaviors are not about embracing what's difficult. The culture of innovation that thrives in Silicon Valley is about unfettered and unrealistic optimism. Because it's common knowledge that North America's West Coast has an unspecified but utterly inevitable date with destiny. The region's appealing landscape of mountains and coast, and indeed the valley itself, was formed by the activity of fault lines that will ultimately do what fault lines do: shift. The most innovative business culture in the world is built on literally shaky ground.

This is no mere coincidence. The seismic instability of the West Coast, combined with its agreeable climate, has produced a live-for-today mentality, a get-it-done-now mind-set. Its relative geographic isolation from most of the population centers of the world has generated a sequestered culture of doing things differently. Into this mix, throw a cluster of intellectual powerhouse universities and the world-class engineering talent they attract, and you get world-changing, investment-attracting innovation.

The point is this: no matter how much we idolize the notion of "visionary," of "change agent," of "risk-taking innovator," the simple fact is that we are not programmed to do it. And because organizations are made up of people, it's even harder for organizations to do it.

Thankfully, although we may be stubbornly committed to comfort and security, we humans are eminently adaptable as a species. And the one instance in which human beings do tend to make dramatic changes is when we have no alternatives. When our individual survival depends on change, change is what we do. Heart attack survivors tend to willingly and immediately alter their diets. Addicts who survive their "rock bottom" event have a greater likelihood of conquering their addiction than those who know they're addicted but haven't experienced the full negative consequences. We'll even change our deeply held beliefs if the circumstance is challenging enough. I know avowed atheists who've admitted to praying their way through a bout of particularly rough in-flight turbulence.

This ability to change in the face of drastic consequences seems less true of organizations. Even when there's clearly no viable alternative, when the strategy is outdated, the business model defunct, and the sales trends inexorably down, most organizations still struggle to adapt.

Adapting

I worked with a company that fell into deep trouble. The firm had been the leader in the mobile technology category for so long that it had lost all organizational memory of how it got there in the first place. It had grown used to enjoying a double-digit share advantage over its closest competitor. As a long-time veteran of the organization once confided to me, "We all used to have cake and champagne every Friday to celebrate how we had beaten our sales targets."

More than ten years of virtually unchallenged growth meant that the company had learned how to be a giant within the context of a particular global environment. It developed a culture of rigorous operational excellence, a focus on maintaining disciplined processes across the whole business. And it fostered a system of decision making based on consensus. By ensuring group input, often bottom-up, on every strategic or operational or talent management choice, it kept things stable.

In this environment, where the company was essentially a machine of operational excellence, employee satisfaction was paramount. Happy workers kept the system humming along smoothly, without tension. Consequently, employee discomfort was grounds for a tough management review. To put it simply, the way things worked was working; in most cases and for years it was working brilliantly. To disrupt the system would have created friction, slowed the production line, and clogged the sales channel. It was a massive engine churning out product and profit. For years.

And then the world changed.

The business experienced a protracted version of a heart attack and a car crash simultaneously. The catalyst: a deadly combination of an outdated software platform, new high-speed and hungry competitors in the business category, and a total redefinition of consumer expectations. It was fascinating to see the difference between the expression of individual perspectives ("We desperately need to do things differently") and the party line on organizational behavior ("But that's just not the way we do it here").

There were, of course, individuals and even board-level leaders who saw potential disaster looming. But even they, with their visionary speeches and dramatic invocations for all to adapt, were not able to guide the company through the necessary transformation.

This is not because they were untalented leaders. In fact, some of the most compelling leaders I have met and worked with were part of this company. The tricky truth is that the clear signs of future profit erosion manifested themselves at a time when sales volume was still far ahead of the closest competitor. The organizational systems were still driving shareholder value, even though its efficacy was about to expire.

Point fingers if you will. But I know of no leading organization that would have done things any differently.

That's because strong organizations have strong cultures, and strong cultures tend to prioritize their continuation, not their adaptation, even in the face of impending disaster. Without the contextual preconditions for constant learning and adaptation, and concrete reward systems in place for new ideas, almost any organization is doomed to fail in the face of dramatic business disruption.

I have often wondered whether the demise of some companies is simply an inevitable and natural occurrence in the larger scheme of things, almost like shifting weather patterns or global immigration shifts. It's certainly painful to be part of a company lurching to keep up. It's even more painful when things don't work out. But once the end happens, the talent (and the patents) can move on to more fertile ground for productivity and value growth.

Still: the reason for this cautionary tale is simple. Whether part of the natural flow or not, demise can be avoided if your organization faces the music early on, and is willing to disrupt its own current success in favor of a future lifespan.

Here's the thing: when an individual "fails" (crashes the car, crashes the marriage, has a sudden life-threatening health crisis) and survives, she is highly likely to adapt. But when an organization fails, it's far less likely that it even *can* survive. And what's more, perhaps it's not even necessary for every organization to survive change. After all, the average lifespan of a company is approximately forty years, less than a human life. The lessons learned will leave the building with its departing talent and be applied elsewhere. A vibrant business ecosystem—and consequently a vibrant economy—is nurtured by disruptive weather patterns of growth and decline and the subsequent redistribution of skills, points of view, talent, experience.

This is not to suggest giving up on organizational change. Far from it. As individuals, as leaders, as citizens, and as family members and participants in life on earth, we have no choice but to aspire to thrive in it. In other words, we must overcome our nature. As individuals first, and then as organizations, and ultimately, as the largest organization there is: all humanity.

Adapting sucks. It's just not fun to move away from what's comfortable. Business is addicted to its current behavior, and why wouldn't it be, when that behavior has been rewarding, at least for business itself. I have seen up close what happens when a society moves on, and a business is unable to cure itself of old habits and outdated assumptions, when it hangs on to those means of generating profit that it knows best, regardless of the signs of decrepitude and ill health that loom. After all, weaning a whole system off its behaviors is even harder than quitting an unhealthy behavior as an individual.

However, the call to action—the desire to make a positive difference in the world—is intensely motivating for individuals. Optimism and passion are infectious, spreading from person to person through conversations, through pride in achievements, and most potently, through the direct experience of the consequences of our actions. Change on a massive scale is far from impossible.

The inspiration to transform our assumptions and our behavior has never been more important than it is right now. We all face a significant moment in our evolution as a species and as stewards of life on earth for future generations.

If it seems utopian to imagine a culture and an economy driven by an inner sense of right and wrong, consider some very obvious examples of conscientious progress.

There was a time when there were no road signs, no international standards for how to travel. There were no speed limits (how fast could your horse go?) and there were no fines for breaking rules that put others' lives at stake. Today, in any developed country, there are recognizable, internationally standardized rules, signs, and symbols that evolved to balance the exigencies of transport with the safety of individuals. There are slight variations between countries, but there are more or less international standards that are intended to protect everyone's well-being.

There was a time not long ago where anyone could smoke anywhere, regardless of the impact on social health systems. It would have been hard to imagine that a movement to curtail the public use of such a profitable and addictive drug would sweep through global capitals. But the sentiment for public well-being prevailed.

There was a time when it made sense to limit knowledge and access to facts to an elite few, who would keep the information to themselves and use it to keep the social infrastructure and economic hierarchy in place. It would have been unthinkable for investors, who enjoyed the benefits of knowledge scarcity, to fund the creation of a technology that provided knowledge abundance to all. Yet it happened. Because in the emerging Culture of Conscience, everyone has the right to all knowledge.

The pace of change is neither slowing nor steadying. It's accelerating. It's built entirely on a shift in our beliefs—about what is important, what is fair, what is good. What we believe is who we become. And that defines—and redefines—everything we do.

This is no overstatement. We only need to look back about two decades, to the dawn of the digital revolution, to remember that a mere evolution of a far older technology—the browser-accessible Internet— thrust business into a new ecology with a new set of rules, and a new lineup of winners and losers. Google did not exist two decades ago. Social media was a seemingly utopian innovation, little more than a headline on a PowerPoint slide, just nine years ago.

From Culture to Economy

Our understanding of the dynamics of the culture we inhabit should never be taken for granted, nor should we assume things to be static and continuous. When culture changes, everything changes with it. Culture instigates economics, not vice versa.

Think about it. You and I have spent our whole lives participating in a system of value exchange that feels predetermined and entrenched. The economy is what the economy is, it would seem. But the means and ways in which trade is conducted are far more mutable than we allow ourselves to believe, even if we accept the notion academically. Money is a human invention. Value and how it is activated and exchanged is contrived. Pre-Columbian people threw tons of gold into a sacred lake; because they had so much of it, its ritual symbolic value was activated by disposing of it (in effect, a form of exchange, albeit with their gods). It was the conquering Spanish who trawled the lake and filled their coffers with their European-assigned value to the commodity. Things hold value because we collectively agree that they do, no more, no less. Value is not intrinsic. It's manufactured. It's belief based.

Perhaps the possibility of allowing ourselves to see the deeper truth—which is that value itself is merely born of assumptions and beliefs—is threatening because it pulls the rug out from under everything we think we know. To consider that we've erected a civilization on sand that is ever shifting can certainly be unnerving. That our business is ultimately reliant on relationships held together by assumptions and beliefs—which of course can change more rapidly than "hard" infrastructure—might seem like a philosophical indulgence rather than an opportunity.

But personally, I find this notion empowering, because it means we can change things for the better. It means that we can and should steer our world. A system that cannot provide for us all fairly and sustainably simply doesn't have to hold dominion over us. And that includes business and how it's conducted.

Culture is at the root of everything we think, say, and do—and that, by definition, includes how and what and why we buy and sell. I'm not using the word "culture" in the sense of artistic sophistication, but in the sense of a totality of commonly held beliefs, ideas, and behaviors. Our culture is, at its most basic, our way of life. And as our way of life changes, that which we value and trade changes too. It's an easy argument to make, but the implications are significant. Because in this era of continuous instability and change, the very nature of business and capital are likely to shift as well. We've grown accustomed to (and perhaps fatigued by) the constant drumbeat on climate change. Less portentous, but equally serious, is the very real possibility of similarly dramatic economic change, driven by the dramatic change in values and beliefs, and the growing power of people to act on their beliefs.

Growing

There is a growing anti-growth movement. (Say that five times fast.) Growth naysayers suggest that growth in the capitalist and economic sense is not viable in the long term because our planet's resources are limited, and is even toxic and dangerous in the short term because the quest for growth promotes ruthless exploitation of natural resources and human beings. They argue that growth as an economic engine and investor motivation is ultimately toxic and outdated, and that it's time to abandon growth as the goal and focus on maintaining balance and equilibrium.

It's not just a radicalized notion, either. The volume of the anti-growth conversation is cranking up, along with its mainstream legitimacy. You hear it at dinner tables, over drinks, and even, sometimes, in corporate conference rooms. It's usually framed as a question, as in: "Is continuous growth really the answer?"

Though its intent may be honorable, I find this concept deeply troubling. To me, there aren't many words or concepts more beautiful and more biomimicry-friendly than growth. Nurture an acorn, and it grows into an oak. Calcium helps our children grow strong. Throughout our lives, we seek to grow in experience and wisdom. Our relationships grow deeper. Our knowledge grows richer. And so on. But of course, cancer grows too. Growth *can* be sinister, and it can kill. So the question is, do we seek value in destructive and exploitative growth, or beneficial and healthy growth? Growth is not something to be *against*. Growth is something to *redefine*.

Take sub-Saharan Africa. What contradictions! Poverty, hunger, conflict, and corruption generate almost unimaginable suffering for many. It's simultaneously replete with virtually untapped human talent and energy, abundant resources, and spectacular natural beauty. Not to mention a dynamic and burgeoning tech start-up scene. Africa's got it all. And do we even need to remind ourselves that it's our ancestral motherland? It's easy to get romantic about the continent, and in a way that's to its detriment. In the United States, in Europe, in many parts of the world, we sum it up, as I just did, as a cliche.

Dynamic growth in Africa actually isn't automatically in the best interests *of* Africa, although it should and could be. At its worst, it sustains the status quo while extracting what's valuable from a financially inexpensive environment and monetizes it overseas. This kind of growth—I'd call it exploitative—doesn't incentivize the region to solve its problems, and I believe it (and every market) can and must be incentivized to solve its own problems; indeed, as long as any region full of resources remains underdeveloped, overhead stays low and foreign profit stays high. Call it an oversimplification and you might be right. But it's the distillation of an uncomfortable truth, and you can apply the business formula in every "emerging" market. We don't like to acknowledge the paradoxical formula of exploitation and aid because it sounds like idealistic (read: unrealistic) hippie stuff, and it all just seems too unsolvable. Meanwhile, we can assuage a bit of nagging guilt with the occasional philanthropic donation or by attending a pop music concert. And anyway, aren't we creating jobs for those people?

But let's take the long view. Can we even envision an Africa that is not an emerging market or a historically troubled set of societies, an Africa that has all the hallmarks of fairness, political stability, health, and knowledge? Put aside for a moment recent projections that suggest it will take more than a generation before most African children will even have a basic education. Put aside the rampant political corruption, deadly tribal conflicts, sexism, and homophobia. What if Africa were the most vibrant marketplace on the planet, a hotbed of new ideas about everything from alternative energy to sustainable agribusiness to entertainment?

Put aside your bias about whether this is realistic or not. Anything is possible. Here's an example: When you read the word *Rwanda,* what do you think about? What picture comes to mind? The answer is usually: genocide and gorillas. You probably do not picture banking, or business at all. The genocide that we associate with the country ended more than twenty years ago. And today, Rwanda's expressed goal is to become the Singapore of Africa, the most business-friendly country in the entire region. It has all but eliminated corruption, and it is attracting billions in investment. It is not a perfect place, but it is a far better place—for Rwandans. Business is the catalyst.

I have intentionally not put a time frame on our African vision, but I'm willing to bet that things will improve faster than most people expect. Lagos is already becoming a hotbed of technology entrepreneurship. (For a glance at the new Africa, just take a look at Co-Creation Hub Nigeria, among other tech incubators.) Because unlike in centuries past, Africa (and every other high-growth market) will not be doing it alone—the pressures and the opportunities of deeper engagement with the global economy will drive its progress. Already, *Forbes* reports that the rate of return on foreign investment in Africa is 9.3 percent, beating both developed nations' and the world average. Indeed, there could well be a time—and who wouldn't hope for it?—when what we used to patronizingly call the Third World and now call High-Growth Economics exceeds their, and our, most hopeful dreams. Obviously, this will be great for citizens of today's impoverished nations. And it will also be great for business. New marketplaces for more products and services. Educated populations become new wellsprings of innovation and entrepreneurship—in health, education, finance, manufacturing, food, water desalination, forestry. I know from years of working in the mobile phone industry that when you solve a problem for people in emerging markets, you create low-cost, high-value innovation that's useful everywhere.

For emerging markets, the journey from today's reality to a happier and healthier scenario is a journey of growth. Growth, with the right motivations and principles in place, is great. It can and must make human lives better while enabling a thriving environment of restorable natural resources.

Optimism needs to be nurtured and managed. It requires an environment in which it is okay to be optimistic even in the face of seemingly impossible challenges. It even needs a bit of healthy magical thinking. It is rooted in faith, and it thrives on the celebration of even the most incremental of wins. Ultimately, it is up to you how you express yourself and how you lead others. If you believe in the power of the Conscience Economy to transform your business and the world for good, you have already taken the first and most crucial step of all. From here on out, it's just another step at a time.

- Be an evangelist for the Conscience Economy. Integrate social and environmental impact into every speech and business statement you make, to employees, to the media, to industry associations. Be as transparent about shortcomings as you are about successes.

- Don't just join one of the array of business consortiums that advocate for social and environmental sensibility, lead one of them. Or create a new and even more visionary one.

- Identify one area of the Conscience Economy where your business can truly stand out from your competition, make it your goal to excel in that area, and do it. It could be anything from sourcing strategy to production to the development of new conscientious business models.

- Establish a cross-functional strategic task force tasked with establishing a Conscience Economy vision for your company, make it accountable to senior management, and rotate your emerging talent through it.

The mass movement for good is great for people. And it's great for resources. And that's ultimately why the Conscience Economy is great for business.

Is there any other option?

Notes

Introduction

A key reading for anyone interested in the intersection of business and society is the seminal work: Milton Friedman, "The Social Responsibility of Business Is to Increase Its Profits," the *New York Times Magazine*, September 13, 1970.

p. xvii: In North America, organic food sales grew in the double digits in the early 2000s and by 9.5 percent in 2011, for example: http://www.nbcnews.com/id/6638417/. At the same time, food sales grew at only 2 to 3 percent http://www.nytimes.com/2005/11/01/business/01organic.html?hp&ex=1130907600&en=1a66fec0344c8870&ei=5094&partner=homepage&_r=0.

p. xxi: A great explanation of the history of the interaction between Quakers, business, and society is available at: http://en.wikipedia.org/wiki/History_of_the_Quakers.

p. xxii: The ideas of Thomas Piketty are explained in the (translated from the French): *Capital in the Twenty-First Century*, Cambridge, MA: Belknap Press, 2014.

Chapter 1

p. 4: For a historical discussion on ubuntu, start with Christian B.N. Gade, "The Historical Development of the Written Discourses on Ubuntu," *South African Journal of Philosophy* 30(3) (2011): 303–329.

p. 9: Steve Jobs's use of LSD is well documented: Yglesias, M. "Steve Jobs told me LSD was a positive life changing experience for me." Last modified June 11, 2012. http://www.slate.com/blogs/moneybox/2012/06/11/steve_jobs_on_lsd_a_positive_life_changing_experience_for_me_.html

p. 9: Other Jiminy Cricket quotes, from Disney's 1940 animated version of *Pinocchio*, are available at the IMDb website: http://www.imdb.com/character/ch0027756/quotes.

p. 10: Of the many Charles Darwin writings, start here: Charles Darwin, *The Descent of Man, and Selection in Relation to Sex* London: Penguin, 2004.

p. 11: From Hannah Arendt's works, start with *Eichmann in Jerusalem: A Report on the Banality of Evil*, 2006, London: Penguin..

p. 14: Ben Thornley's post is here: Thornley, B "The Facts on US Social Enterprise." Last modified 8 Nov 2012. "http://www.huffingtonpost.com/ben-thornley/social-enterprise_b_2090144.html.

Chapter 2

p. 23: On biohacking: Alessandro Delfanti, *Biohackers: The Politics of Open Science* (New York: Pluto Press, 2013) and Craig Venter, *Life at the Speed of Light* (New York: Penguin Group, 2013).

p. 24: On conflict: Steven Pinker, *The Better Angels of Our Nature: A History of Violence and Humanity* (London: Penguin Group, 2012).

p. 25: On obesity: Cynthia J. Stein and Graham A. Colditz, "The Epidemic of Obesity," *The Journal of Clinical Endocrinology and Metabolism*, Vol 89, No.6, (2004): 2522–2525.

p. 24: On the decline in globalviolence: Mack, A. 2014. "The Decline in Global Violence." Accessed August 2014 http://www.factsandopinions.com/galleries/expert-witness/the-decline-in-global-violence/ and Simon Fraser, *Human Security Report 2013, The Decline in Global Violence: Evidence, Explanation and Contestation* (Vancouver: Human Security Press, 2013).

p. 25: On computers and human thinking: Raymond Kurzweil, *The Singularity Is Near* (New York: Penguin Group, 2005).

p. 26: Cadwalladr, C. "Are the robot's about to rise? Google's new director of engineering thinks so…" Last modified 22 Feb 2014. http://www.theguardian.com/technology/2014/feb/22/robots-google-ray-kurzweil-terminator-singularity-artificial-intelligence.

p. 26: The Futurist. "Timing the Singularity" Accessed August 2014. http://www.singularity2050.com/2009/08/timing-the-singularity.html.

p. 27: On nanotechnology, a primer: nanowerk "graphene—properties, uses, and applications" Accessed August 2014. http://www.nanowerk.com/spotlight/spotid=34184.php and Sargent Jr, J. 2013 *Nanotechnology: A Policy*

Primer (Congressional Research Service Report) http://www.bespacific.com/crs-nanotechnology-a-policy-primer-2/

Chapter 3

p. 43: For Maslow's hierarchy: Abraham Maslow, A *Motivation and Personality* 2nd ed. (New York: Harper and Row, 1970).

p. 47: On US energy: US Energy Information Administration. "Energy Perspectives 1949-2011" Last modified 27 September, 2012. http://www.eia.gov/totalenergy/data/annual/perspectives.cfm and "Annual Energy Review." Accessed August 2014 http://www.eia.gov/totalenergy/data/annual/

p. 48: The history of *Wired* magazine is as recalled by the author, who worked for the magazine at the time.

p. 50: On outcome prediction: Malcolm Gladwell, *Blink* (London: Penguin Group, 2012).

p. 54: If you're interested in more about the history of the social enterprise restaurant Fifteen: "About Fifteen," 2014, Jamie Oliver Food Foundation, http://www.jamieoliver.com/the-fifteen-apprentice-programme/about/story.

p. 54: The statistics concerning impact investing and social enterprise are debatable and evolving. For a starting point, the following resource may be of use: GIIN. "Perspectives on Progress" Accessed August 2014. http://www.thegiin.org/cgi-bin/iowa/resources/research/489.html.

p. 58: On India and impact investing: Singh, N. "India takes centre stage in impact investing" Last modified 10 Jun 2013. http://timesofindia.indiatimes.com/business/india-business/India-takes-centre-stage-in-impact-investing/articleshow/20512517.cms

p. 57: On philanthropy: "Philanthropy 50—A Look at the 50 Most Generous Donors of 2013, *The Chronicle of Philanthropy,* 2014, http://philanthropy.com/article/A-Look-at-the-50-Most-Generous/144529/#p50_list.

Chapter 4

p. 67: Some commentary on Barilla is available here: Sieczkowski, C. "Barilla Pasta won't feature gay families in Ads, says critics can eat another brand of pasta" Last modified 26 Sep 2013. http://www.huffingtonpost.com/2013/09/26/barilla-pasta-anti-gay_n_3995679.html

p. 79: Timothy M.Devinney, P. Auger, and Giana M. Eckhardt, *The Myth of the Ethical Consumer* (New York: Cambridge University Press, 2010).

p. 81: Andrew Grove, *Only the Paranoid Survive* (London: Profile Books Ltd., 1997).

Chapter 5

p. 88: For the social conscience survey, see *Fortune* magazine, 1946.

p. 88: The phases discussed in this chapter are from: Patrick E. Murphy, "An Evolution: Corporate Social Responsiveness," *University of Michigan Business Review*, Vol 30, No.6 (1978).

Chapter 6

p. 104: Peter F. Drucker, *The Practice of Management* (New York: Harper & Row Publications Ltd., 1954).

On values-based business: Jim Collins and Jerry I. Porras, *Built to Last: Successful Habits of Visionary Companies* (New York: HarperCollins, 2002).

A classic on building long-term brand value: David A. Aaker, *Building Strong Brands* (New York: Free Press, 1996).

Chapter 7

p. 118: Creative abrasion is referred to in D. Leonard-Barton and W. Swap, *When Sparks Fly: Igniting Creativity in Groups* (Cambridge, MA: Harvard Business School Press, 1999).

p. 123: On crowdsourcing and crowdfunding: Enrique Estelles-Arolas and Fernando González-Ladrón-de-Guevara, "Towards an Integrated Crowdsourcing Definition," *Journal of Information Science*, Vol 38, No.2. (2012): 189–200 and Ethan Mollick, "The Dynamics of Crowdfunding: An Exploratory Study," *Journal of Business Venturing*, Vol 29, Issue 1 (2014): 1–16

A key work on collaboration: Charles Leadbeater, *We-Think: Mass Innovation Not, Mass Production* (London: Profile Books, 2008).

Chapter 8

p. 134: Milton Friedman, "The Social Responsibility of Business Is to Increase Its Profits," the *New York Times Magazine*, September 13, 1970.

p. 134: George Marshall, "The Marshall Plan" (speech, Harvard University, Cambridge, MA, June 5, 1947), http://www.oecd.org/general/themarshallplan speechatharvarduniversity5june1947.htm.

p. 136: The invisible hand: Adam Smith, *The Theory of Moral Sentiments* (London: A.Millar, 1759).

p. 138: For global data on consumer trust by business sector, consult Kantar Group's annual Global Monitor and BrandZ reports, London. [**Au: available how? where? can you provide a link or some direction?**]

p. 139: An overview of Six Sigma can be found here: Roger G. Schroeder, Kevin Linderman, Charles Liedtke, and Adrian S. Choo, "Six Sigma: Definition and Underlying Theory," *Journal of Operations Management,* Vol 26, Issue 4 (2008): 536–554 or at Wikipedia's entry for Six Sigma, http://en.wikipedia.org/wiki/Six_Sigma.

p. 140: For the Sullivan principles, see the Wikipedia entry the Sullivan principles, http://en.wikipedia.org/wiki/Sullivan_principles. For more on the Equator Principles, start with the website of the Equator Principles Association: http://www.equator-principles.com/. And for the Principles for Responsible Investment, visit the PRI Association website: http://www.unpri.org/.

p. 141: Of the many works by Nassim Taleb, start with: Nassim N. Taleb, *Antifragile: Things That Gain from Disorder* (London: Penguin Group, 2012).

p. 144: For integrated reporting: http://www.theiirc.org/ For triple bottom line, start with: Timothy F. Slaper and Tanya J. Hall, "The Triple Bottom Line: What Is It and How Does It Work?" *Indiana Business Review,* Vol 86, No.1 (2011): 4–8.

Chapter 9

p. 157: Shaw's quote is from: George B. Shaw, *Maxims for Revolutionists* (New York: Cambridge University Press, 1903).

p. 163: For more on gold and lakes, see the Metropolitan Museum of Art *Bulletin*, New York, Spring 2002.

p. 165: A seminal and useful work on future scenario planning: Peter Schwartz, *The Art of the Long View: Planning for the Future in an Uncertain World* (New York: Doubleday/Currency, 1991).

p. 166: The Co-Creation Hub's website is here: http://cchubnigeria.com/.

p. 166: On Africa's rate of return: Strauss, Karsen. "Let's build a tech startup in…Rwanda?" Last modified 1 April 2014. http://www.forbes.com/sites/karstenstrauss/2014/04/01/lets-build-a-tech-startup-in-rwanda/

References

The Conscience Economy was broadly informed by a range of books, papers, articles, and conversations. Many of my assertions are based on the sum of my own experiences working across a range of business sectors, and I take full responsibility (and blame) for them! However, there are particular works that have had considerable influence on my thinking, and in this section I set out some of the readings and source material that I've found both informative and provocative. In deference to the discussion in many of the chapters of the book about the efficacy of online collaboration, I have referenced Wikipedia and other online information throughout—no doubt by the time you read this, the resources to be found online will be even better!

Amini, Amrollah, Mostafa Emami, and Alireza Emami. "Corporate Social Responsibility Risk and Return in Portfolio Management." *International Conference on Management Research and Advances in Accounting* (2014): 1–28.

Baumgartner, Rupert J., and Daniela Ebner. "Corporate Sustainability Strategies: Sustainability Profiles and Maturity Levels." *Sustainable Development* 18 (2010): 76–89.

Blazovich, Janell L., and Murphy L. Smith. "Ethical Corporate Citizenship: Does it Pay?" *Research on Professional Responsibility and Ethics in Accounting* (2010): 1–42.

Chatterji, Aaron K., D. I. Levine, and Michael W. Toffel. "How Well Do Social Ratings Actually Measure Corporate Social Responsibility?" *Journal of Economics and Management Strategy,* Vol 18, Issue 1 (2009): 125–169.

Choi, Gilbert, and Jaesoek Ha. "Socially Responsible Investment in the Spotlight." *Issue Analysis* (2013): 1–15.

Christensen, Clayton M., Dina Wang, and Derek Van Bever. "Consulting on the Cusp of Disruption." *Harvard Business Review* (2013): 106–150.

Dyllick, Thomas, and Kai Hockerts. "Beyond the Business Case for Corporate Sustainability." *Business Strategy and the Environment* 11 (2002): 130–141.

Ferguson, Lindsey. "Gaining (from) Your Clients' Trust." *Journal of Accountancy* (2012): 38–43.

Flammer, Caroline. "Does Corporate Social Responsibility Lead to Superior Financial Performance? A Regression Discontinuity Approach." (2013): 1–27.

Gray, Rob, and Jan K. Bebbington. "Corporate Sustainability: Accountability and the Pursuit of the Impossible Dream." In *Handbook of Sustainable Development,* edited by Giles Atkinson, Simon Dietz, and Eric Neumayer. London: Edward Elgar, 2007.

Hahn, Tobias, Frank Figge, Jonatan Pinkse, and Lutz Preuss. "Trade-Offs in Corporate Sustainability: You Can't Have Your Cake and Eat It." *Business Strategy and the Environment* 19 (2010): 217–229.

Hanson, Kirk O. "The Long History of Conscious Capitalism." *California Management Review,* Vol 53, No.3 (2011): 77–82.

Henisz, Witold J., Sinziana Dorobantu, and Lite Nartey. "Spinning Gold: The Financial Returns to External Stakeholder Engagement." *Strategic Management Journal* (2011): 1–40.

Holme, Charles. "Corporate Social Responsibility: A Strategic Issue or a Wasteful Distraction?" *Industrial and Commercial Training,* Vol 42, No.4 (2010): 179–185.

Idowu, Samuel O. "An Exploratory Study of the Historical Landscape of Corporate Social Responsibility in the UK." *Corporate Governance: The International Journal of Business in Society,* Vol 11, No.2 (2011): 149–160.

KPMG. "KPMG International Survey of Corporate Responsibility Reporting 2011." *KPMG International Cooperative* (2011): 1–34.

Kraus, Patrick, and Bernd Brititzelmaier. "A Literature Review on Corporate Social Responsibility: Definitions, Theories and Recent Empirical Research." *International Journal of Management Cases* (2012): 282–296.

Linnenluecke, Martina K., Sally V. Russell, and Andrew Griffiths. "Subcultures and Sustainability Practices: The Impact on Understanding Corporate Sustainability." *Business Strategy and the Environment* 18 (2009): 432–452.

Lys, Thomas, James Naughton, and Clare Wang. "Pinpointing the Value in CSR." *Public-Private Interface* (2013): 1–5.

Madrakhimova, Firuza S. "Evolution of the Concept and Definition of Corporate Social Responsibility." *Global Conference on Business and Finance Proceedings,* Vol 8, No.2 (2013): 113–118.

McElhaney, Kellie. "A Strategic Approach to Corporate Social Responsibility." *Leader to Leader* (2009): 30–36.

McWilliams, Abagail, and Donald Siegel. "Corporate Social Responsibility and Financial Performance: Correlation or Misspecification?" *Strategic Management Journal* 21 (2000): 603–609.

Renneboog, Luc, Jenke Ter Horst, and Chendi Zhang. "Socially Responsible Investments: Institutional Aspects, Performance, and Investor Behavior." *Journal of Banking and Finance* 32 (2008): 1723–1742.

Tsoutsoura, Margarita. "Corporate Social Responsibility and Financial Performance." *University of California, Berkeley, Working Paper* (2004): 1–21.

Vanhamme, Joëlle, and Bas Grobben. "Too Good to Be True! The Effectiveness of CSR History in Countering Negative Publicity." *Journal of Business Ethics* 85 (2009): 273–283.

Van Liedekerke, Luc, and Wim Dubbink. "Twenty Years of European Business Ethics—Past Developments and Future Concerns." *Journal of Business Ethics* 82 (2008): 273–280.

Van Marrewijk, Marcel, and Marco Were. "Multiple Levels of Corporate Sustainability." *Journal of Business Ethics* 44 (2003): 107–119.

Vázquez-Carrasco, Rosario, and Eugenia M. López-Pérez. "Small and Medium-Sized Enterprises and Corporate Social Responsibility: A Systematic Review of the Literature." *Quality and Quantity* (2012): 3205–3218.

Villeneuve-Smith, Frank, and Charlotte Chung. "Social Enterprise UK. The People's Business." *Social Enterprise UK* (2013): 1–44.

Visser, Wayne. "The Future of CSR: Towards Transformative CSR, or CSR 2.0." *Kaleidoscope Futures Paper Series* (2012): 1–17.

Zhou, S., Xiaohong Quan, and William Jiang. "Corporate Social Responsibility and Sustainable Development in China: Literature Review and Case Analysis." *Journal of Supply Chain and Operations Management,* Vol 10, No.1 (2012): 54–64.

Index

Acknowledgments

I'm not the first to say it: creating a book is indeed a labor of love, an ongoing collaborative process of conversation, debate, research, and physical nurture. I will be forever grateful for the care and continual egging-on from so many colleagues and friends, more than I can mention. But I'm compelled to shout out a few, without whose support I might have resorted to simply tweeting haikus of 140 characters, and speechifying in twenty-minute segments, rather than committing tens of thousands of words and countless hours of thought and analysis to the subject.

Muchas, muchas gracias to Kevin Allen, my mentor and dear friend, who nudged me from thinking into authoring. To Andy Bird, who calmly listened and counseled throughout. To my team of brilliant EMBA candidates at the Cambridge Judge Business School who helped me form the thesis while researching its dimensions: Lenore Gerschwitz, Shreyas Derashri, Adebowale Adeleke, Sara O'Donavan, and especially to Richard Wheater, who personally and fearlessly dove into my first draft and made it better. To Amooti Binaisa, whose irrepressible encouragement (and songs at the piano) spurred me on. To Suzette and Jeff Clarke, who believed in the Conscience Economy from the moment I first dropped it into conversation, and whose economic and journalistic rigor gave the argument shape. To Dick and Teresa Alpert, who nourished my thinking and my stomach whenever I needed either. To Louis Rossetto, who early on offered two pieces of guiding wisdom I try to follow every day: always fail upward and always write about the future, not the past. To Marcos and the crew at Satan's Coffee Corner in Barcelona, who kept me upbeat and caffeinated throughout my writing in exile. To my editors and book-creation sherpas Erika Heilman and Susan Lauzau, whose blend of empathy, foresight, and strategic smarts made the whole process feel more like a dance than work. To my mom and dad, whose commitment to living sensibly and loving authentically both inspires me and keeps my feet on the ground.

Most of all, thank you to my partner in life, Mark Atkinson, who has always lived in the Conscience Economy and showed me the way.

About the Author

Steven Overman works on the frontline of business and culture transformation, helping teams deliver new ideas that generate billions of dollars of economic value while positively changing the lives of people everywhere.

He was one of the earliest members of the group that created and spread the message of the Digital Revolution at *Wired* magazine, even collaborating on the invention of the ad banner for the world's first commercial website Hotwired (an early offshoot of Wired.) He helped create the Academy Award-winning movie *Philadelphia*, which transformed the global conversation about HIV/AIDS. He led the international launch of the world's first smartphone, the blockbuster Nokia N95, and created innovative marketing for a whole new category of affordable mobile technology that connected a billion new consumers to the internet, from India to Indonesia to Sub-Saharan Africa.

As a strategy and innovation consultant for startups as well as Fortune 100 companies across a range of industry sectors, and during his tenure as Vice President of Global Brand and Marketing Creation for Nokia Corporation, Steven has collaborated with a broad range of leaders from the C-suite to the product and software design studio, from the R&D lab to the patent department. He has pored over state-of-the-art market research and consumer insight from nearly every corner of the globe, collaborated with the world's leading creative studios and advertising agencies, developed future scenarios for the shipping and logistics industry, imagined and evangelized concepts for sustainable hospitality and sustainability infrastructure for international brands, co-created award-winning youth marketing in countries and cultures around the world, and mentored young entrepreneurs. A frequent public speaker, guest academic lecturer, and business leadership advisor, Steven is based in London.